Sketches of Bird Life

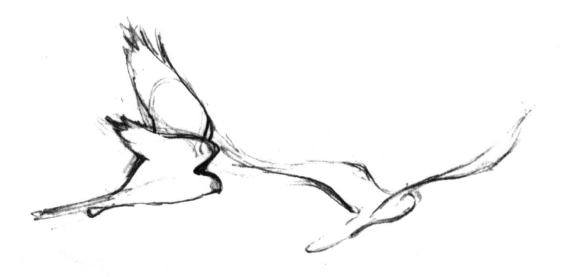

C.F. Tunnicliffe R.A.
Sketches of Bird Life

Introduction and commentary by Robert Gillmor

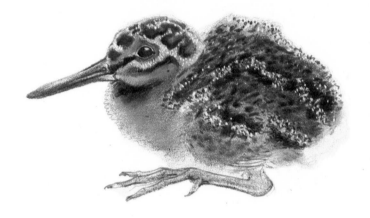

NATIONWIDE BOOK SERVICE

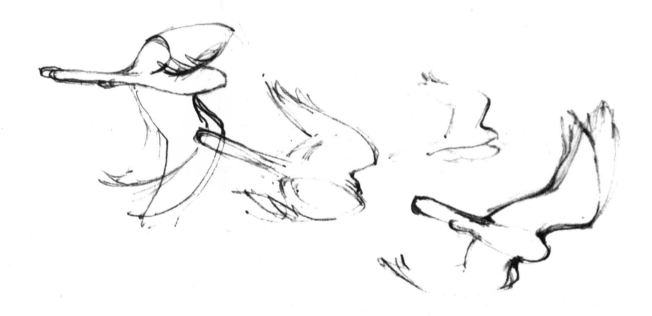

This edition published 1981
by Nationwide Book Service
by arrangement with
Victor Gollancz Ltd

Printed in Italy by
A. Mondadori Editore, Verona

Contents

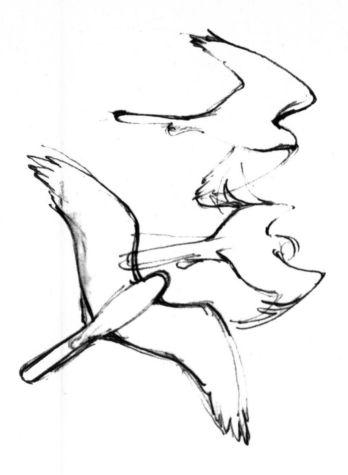

The pencil sketches on this and other preliminary pages are taken from a page of studies of Hen Harrier *Circus cyaneus*.

The drawing on the title-page is of a young Snipe *Capella gallinago*.

Introduction

It was during my impressionable early teens that Charles Tunnicliffe's more important bird illustrations were being published. I shall never forget my excitement when shown a copy of *Our Bird Book*, at the home of a friend's aunt and, eventually, on receiving my own copy from an indulgent grandmother. I had also been given *Bird Portraiture* and in the next few years came *Mereside Chronicle*, *Birds of the Estuary* and, finest of all, *Shorelands Summer Diary*. His birds seemed so full of life, so right, so obviously done from first hand observation that they took my breath away. Nearly thirty years later I was to experience the same sensation when presented with two large cardboard boxes containing over fifty of Charles Tunnicliffe's sketchbooks. All the old excitement returned as I opened a book and became lost amongst the birds of the Anglesey seabird colonies and the daily goings on at Cob Lake. To select a few pages from so many demanding inclusion seemed an almost impossible task. I soon realised that it was important to reveal something of the rich variety of drawings in the sketchbooks, and I wanted to give priority to sketches showing aspects of bird behaviour and birds in action. My final selection is also intended to demonstrate how a great bird artist sketched with purpose, to produce material he could work from later, and how important were his annotations to the drawings. In this respect I hope that the many people who are keen to add to their interest in birds by learning about drawing them, will find this book of use and inspiration.

Tunnicliffe's own interest in birds started when he was preparing illustrations for an edition of Henry Williamson's book *The Peregrine's Saga* (1934) which he considered had a marked influence on the future trend of his work. He joined a meet of members of the Falconry Club while they were flying their hawks at Avebury and described this as ". . . a really good experience of bird study because . . . when the hawks were resting, I was allowed to go amongst them . . .". We know he was already strongly attracted to birds for their aesthetic possibilities and it seems likely that this early opportunity to study birds at close quarters showed him their practical possibilities. He found this experience with the falconers invaluable and, as he said, "One thing leads to another and birds led to birds."

A year or so later he visited Iona, in the Inner Hebrides, and fell under its spell. It was here that his new interest in birds was confirmed. In *My Country Book* he wrote: "This visit, I think, was the real start of serious bird study, for after that I concentrated more and more on the birds of my native countryside, and especially those of the Cheshire meres. Sketch book after sketch book became filled with studies for bird pictures, and later my happy hunting grounds extended as far afield as Pembroke and Sutherland."

It was when working on engravings for *A Book of Birds* (1937) by Mary Priestley, the first book entirely on birds he had been asked to illustrate, that Tunnicliffe sought advice from an outstanding ornithologist, Reg Wagstaffe, who was curator of Stockport Museum. They became friends and Tunnicliffe described him as ". . . an excellent field man and an excellent museum man." Wagstaffe gave Tunnicliffe an insight into the importance of a scientific approach and the importance of accurate identification. In Tunnicliffe's own words: "He gave me my first breaking-in as far as science was concerned." His studies of dead birds, measured to a millimetre and most accurately coloured, were part of Tunnicliffe's answer to the problem of learning exactly what birds look like. In making these drawings he not only taught himself a great deal about birds themselves but provided himself with references to which he could turn at any time. He regarded them as scientific studies and they were very important to him. "Every bird that comes into my hand," he said, ". . . is measured and drawn from all possible angles so that the feather map, as we call it, is complete."

Although Tunnicliffe described these drawings somewhat

dismissively as "feather maps" he was too great an artist for them to be mere diagrams. They are beautifully composed and painted and form a major part of his artistic output. For an example, see number **90**. On one occasion while discussing these drawings, he said: "But, of course, all this drawing of fine detail and actual measurement of the species is but the measurement of the species; the next thing is to particularize the bird that you want to draw—to get the real essence of the bird . . .". Getting the real essence is the challenge faced by every artist. Getting the individual character of a bird requires many hours of patient fieldwork and Tunnicliffe's crowded sketchbooks reveal his success at this and also his passion for studying the living bird. He steadily built up this great collection of reference material—live and dead studies—which eventually produced an almost inexhaustible supply of ideas for paintings and illustrations.

While Tunnicliffe's writing is perfectly legible, the annotations which accompany the sketches are not always easy to read on the printed page, especially as some were written in a rather small hand and crammed into a narrow space along the edge of the page. These are of such interest that I have transcribed them and they are printed in italics in the captions. The annotations nearly always contain the basic information of species, date and place where seen. There are often additional notes on the sex and age of the bird and, where appropriate, the weather or light conditions and time of day. When some aspect of behaviour has been drawn a detailed account is usually added, perhaps at considerable length, and the sequence of actions carefully noted. He often supplemented the drawing with a written description of the colour and plumage pattern of the bird, as in the drawing of a pair of Redshanks, number **23**. The books which Tunnicliffe wrote were full of illustrations making use of the material in his sketchbooks. Looking through the sketchbooks I frequently came across evidence of this. Some examples are reproduced here, together with the relevant passages of text from Tunnicliffe's writings, see for example numbers **32** and **33**. As well as the annotations these quotations are printed in italics in the captions and the sources acknowledged.

Tunnicliffe's early sketchbooks were mostly small commercial books, usually upright in shape with many pages of white paper in which he drew with pencil, pen and crayon—the paper being too thin for paint. Later he had sketchbooks made up to his own design and bound at Manchester Grammar School where he assisted the art master during the war. He used these hand bound books to the end of his life, especially in the studio where he worked up his field sketches after a day in the field. They were made up from sheets of stout watercolour paper of different tones and colours, the paintings being done on the one side of the paper only. I confess that seeing them bound in familiar materials—the same that I had used in my own bookbinding classes at school in the early fifties—gave me particular pleasure. In the field he continued to use books of white paper of no special quality but perfectly adequate for the soft pencil drawings which he made at great speed, capturing poses with bold unfussy lines, seldom labouring a drawing but starting anew when the model moved to a fresh position. For examples, see numbers **6**, **42** and **46**.

Although birds predominate, the sketchbooks contain much else besides. Some consist almost entirely of landscapes and studies of buildings, boats and figures. In others there are farm and domestic animals, zoo studies, insects, fish, the occasional mammal met in the field and numerous fancy pigeons. There are also many detailed sketches of bird habitats, storing information for use later when composing the settings for paintings and illustrations.

Tunnicliffe was a master painter of water in all its moods, from the still pool with mirror reflections of Grebe or Pintail to surging seas with parties of Eider riding the switchback waves. There are studies of water surfaces, drawings capturing the complex oily rippling of water disturbed by a breeze or the flow of a fast, rock-strewn stream where a Dipper or Grey Wagtail might be found.

For many people the peak of Tunnicliffe's art was reached in his major watercolour paintings. He regarded the six large pictures produced for the Royal Academy each year as the culmination of all the study and preparation in the field and studio, of which the sketches were perhaps the most vital part. They were greatly superior to much of his more widely known work done for commercial outlets where, because subtleties of tone and colour are easily lost in the process of colour reproduction, he tended to paint with a much brighter palette.

Tunnicliffe devoted his life to his art, working unceasingly for over fifty years. The sketches, measured drawings, prints and paintings are evidence of a loving but entirely unsentimental obsession by a man who was recognised by many in his lifetime as one of the most considerable artists to have drawn inspiration from the British countryside and its wildlife. It is good to know that all the sketchbooks and measured drawings will be kept together in a permanent home on Anglesey. There they may be seen, studied and enjoyed by those already familiar with Tunnicliffe's work; others will journey there to discover for themselves the work of a master craftsman and artist who reflects the deepest feelings in people for a natural world not dominated by chemicals and concrete.

Reading, Berkshire
June 1981

Charles Frederick Tunnicliffe,
O.B.E., R.A.

CHRONOLOGY

1901   Born 1st December, Langley, Cheshire, to William and Margaret Tunnicliffe.

1903   Family move to Lane Ends Farm. Attends St James's School, Sutton.

1915–21   Macclesfield and Manchester Schools of Art.

1921–25   Royal College of Art, London (Royal Exhibition Scholarship).

1923   Awarded R.C.A. Painting School Diploma, with distinction.

1924   Joins the R.C.A. Engraving School.

1925   Joins staff of Woolwich Polytechnic.

1925   William Tunnicliffe dies, June.

1928   Two etchings accepted for Royal Academy Summer Exhibition, his first submission.

1928   Leaves London to return to Cheshire.

1929   Marries Winifred Wonnacott at Whalley Range and settles in Macclesfield.

1929   Elected to Membership of the Manchester Academy of Fine Art.

1932   Illustrated edition of *Tarka the Otter* by Henry Williamson published.

1934   One wood engraving accepted for Royal Academy Summer Exhibition. Exhibits there every year thereafter to 1978.

1934   Elected Fellow of Royal Society of Painter–Etchers and Engravers.

1937   *A Book of Birds* by Mary Priestley, with 81 wood engravings, published.

1938   One-man Exhibition at the Arthur Greatorex Galleries, London, of bird paintings on unprimed cloth.

1939–45   Assistant Art Master at Manchester Grammar School.

1942   *My Country Book* published. The first of his own books.

1944   Elected Associate of the Royal Academy of Arts.

1945   *Bird Portraiture* published.

1947   27th March, Charles and Winifred move to Malltraeth, Anglesey.

1947   *How to draw Farm Animals* published.

1947   *Our Bird Book* published (with Sydney Rogerson).

1948   *Mereside Chronicle* published.

1949   *Both Sides of the Road* published (with Sydney Rogerson).

1950   Paints his first Christmas card for the Royal Society for the Protection of Birds.

1952   *Shorelands Summer Diary* published.

1952   *Birds of the Estuary* published.

1954   Elected Royal Academician.

1954   Elected a Vice-President of the R.S.P.B.

1954–66   Paints every cover for the R.S.P.B. journal *Bird Notes*.

1968   Accepts invitation to be a Vice-President of the Society of Wildlife Artists.

1969   Winifred Tunnicliffe dies, May.

1974   Exhibition of *Bird Drawings*, Diploma Galleries, Royal Academy of Arts, 3rd August to 29th September.

1975   Awarded Gold Medal of the R.S.P.B. for services to bird protection.

1978   Awarded Order of the British Empire in the Queen's Birthday Honours, 3rd June.

1979   Dies 7th February, Malltraeth, Anglesey.

1979   Memorial Exhibits at Royal Academy Summer Exhibition and Society of Wildlife Artists Annual Exhibition.

1979   *A Sketchbook of Birds* published.

1980   *Portrait of a Country Artist* by Ian Niall, published.

1980   *Wild Lives. The Art of Charles F. Tunnicliffe.* A retrospective Exhibition held at the Mostyn Art Gallery, Llandudno, 9th August to 20th September, and National Museum of Wales, Cardiff, 7th to 23rd November.

Courtship and display

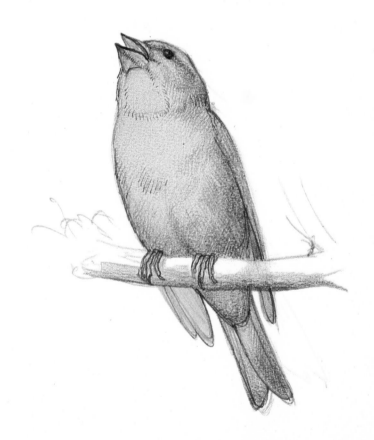

Apart from man, birds have the most highly developed vocal language of any animal group and, along with their powers of flight, the songs and calls of birds have made us notice them in a way that is unique in the animal kingdom. The Sedge Warbler opposite is in full song, at the time of year when the males are establishing territories and singing in order to warn other males to keep away. At the same time they hope to attract the females which usually return from their winter quarters in Africa some days later. Song can threaten and warn off potential rivals without the need for actual fighting; it also acts as a sexual display, helping in pair formation as well as in maintaining the pair bond.

Songbirds usually sing from a perch which gives them prominence within the territory and from which they have a good all-round view. It is also a way of marking the area of the territory as they sing from perches around its border. Skylarks, living in open country without high songposts, sing in flight, high above the ground, the song cascading with hardly a pause. Occasionally they use a perch and the Skylark (**16**) Tunnicliffe sketched at Goldsitch Moss one April, poured forth song while perched on a wall. Song is therefore of fundamental importance to some species whereas others, with a much reduced vocal range, use more visual methods of communication. Signals are given, usually in ritualised movements and often involving the display of boldly patterned or brightly coloured plumage. A good example of

elaborate courtship display is the Mandarin (**6** and **7**): the brilliantly coloured drake has special features of head plumes and enlarged inner secondary feathers which he shows off to the best advantage in a series of postures. Tunnicliffe described and drew the Mandarins displaying on a visit to the Wildfowl Trust at Slimbridge. Other duck displays were watched nearer home and one of the species he observed was Goldeneye. The drake is not particularly colourful but the plumage is boldly marked black and white; the black, green glossed head shows off the bright yellow eyes and white cheek patches. From his studio window, one cold February morning, he saw a small flock of Goldeneye on the river. Several drakes were posturing before a duck and he made a fine studio sketch afterwards (**9**).

Most wading birds conduct their courtship within the pair and Tunnicliffe's long series of notes and sketches of a pair of Ringed Plover going through part of their display (**2–4**) is a typical example of his careful observation. Some waders are more social and will display in groups, like the piping party of Oystercatchers (**14**). These two pairs may well have been patrolling an adjacent boundary of their respective territories, the noisy display helping to fix the demarcation line to their mutual satisfaction. The Avocet sketches (**10–13**) were made in 1950 when Tunnicliffe went to Suffolk specially to make drawings of this elegant wader's courtship displays.

Previous page: Greenfinch *Chloris chloris*.

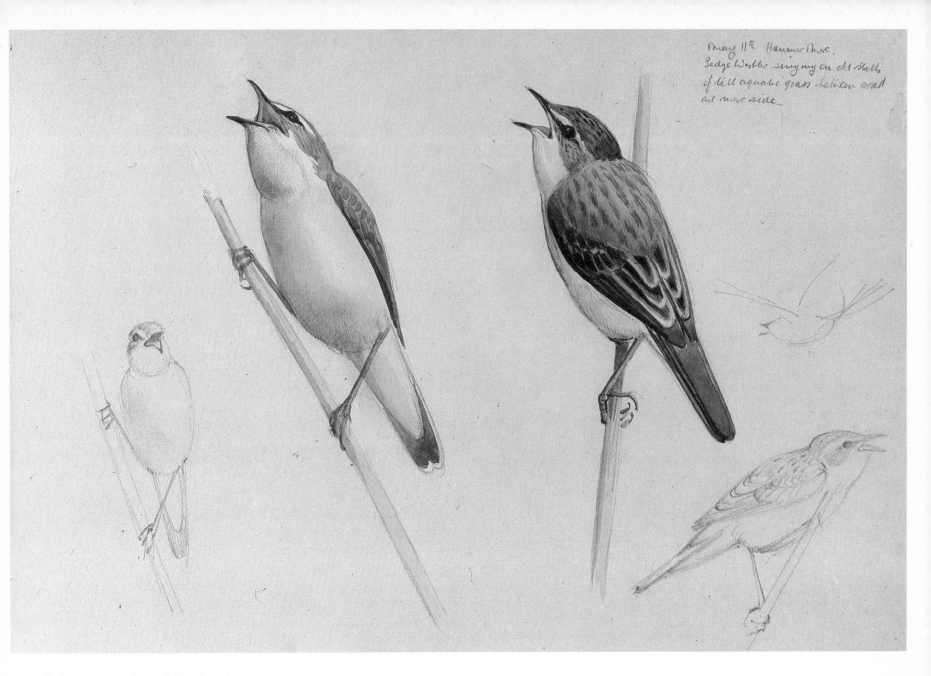

1 Sedge Warbler *Acrocephalus schoenobaenus*,
Hanmer Mere, May 11th 1947.

*Singing on old stalks of tall aquatic grass between road
and mereside.*

2 Ringed Plover *Charadrius hiaticula*, Menai Straits, April 11th 1954.

Two Ring Plover resting on the stones of the upper beach. Almost invisible against the stones. Presently the male moved, stalked a little distance, then squatted. Moved again over the stones and then squatted in a depression, and, breast down, wing tips slightly up and tail slightly depressed he kicked with his feet (2). Calling all the time. He scraped several times in this way. Then Turnstones came feeding over the beach and the male attacked the nearest birds with a rush, tail depressed and fanned out, and neck swollen, body in a crouch (3). Sometimes the Turnstones ran away, at other times they ignored the attacks, and once or twice they retaliated and lunged at the R. Plover. Again he went to his scraping, calling all the time, and between bouts of kicking he stood and flung tiny pebbles or bits of shell to the side and behind him. On two occasions when he had scraped in a hollow he stood on the edge of the hollow and the female ran to him. He adopted a stiff slightly bowed attitude with a wing half open and tail depressed and projecting over the hollow. The female ran to him, down into the hollow under his wing and tail, and came up on the other side (4). Then each separated, and presently the female went along the beach and sank into a hollow and began to scrape. He approached her and then both stood for a second or so, close together with tails depressed (5). He went into the scraping position frequently and when this action terminated he invariably had a bout of pebble or shell throwing. The cock bird much the more active of the two.

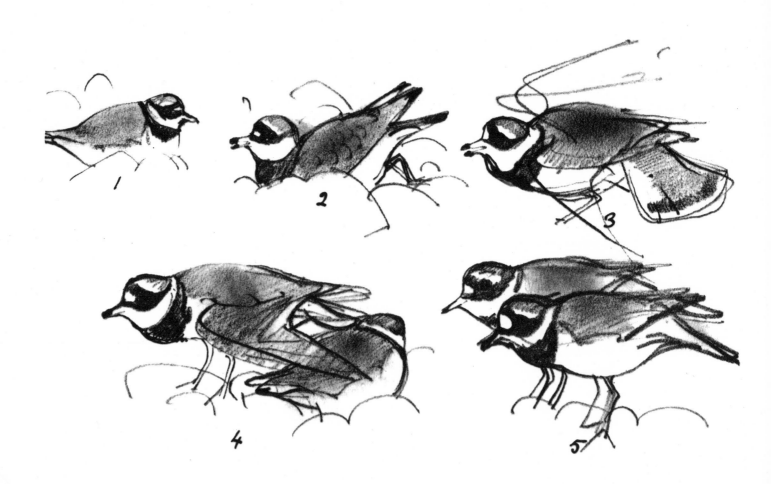

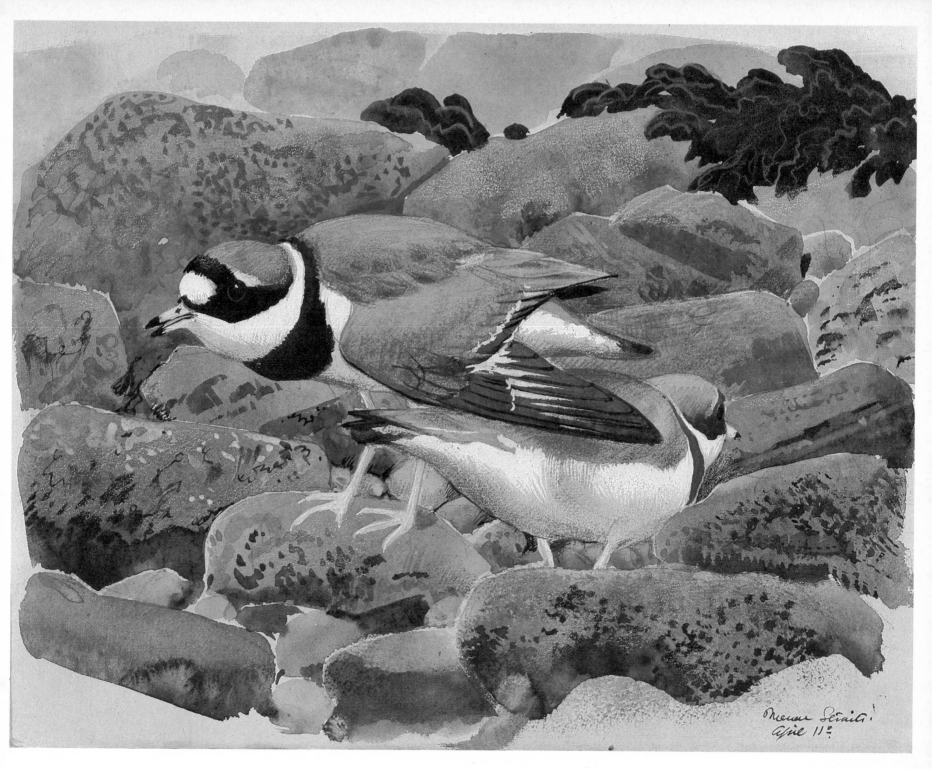

3 Ringed Plover *Charadrius hiaticula*, Menai Straits,
April 11th 1954.

A watercolour drawing, made in the studio, using
the notes and field sketches opposite, of a pair of
Ringed Plovers during part of their courtship
display.

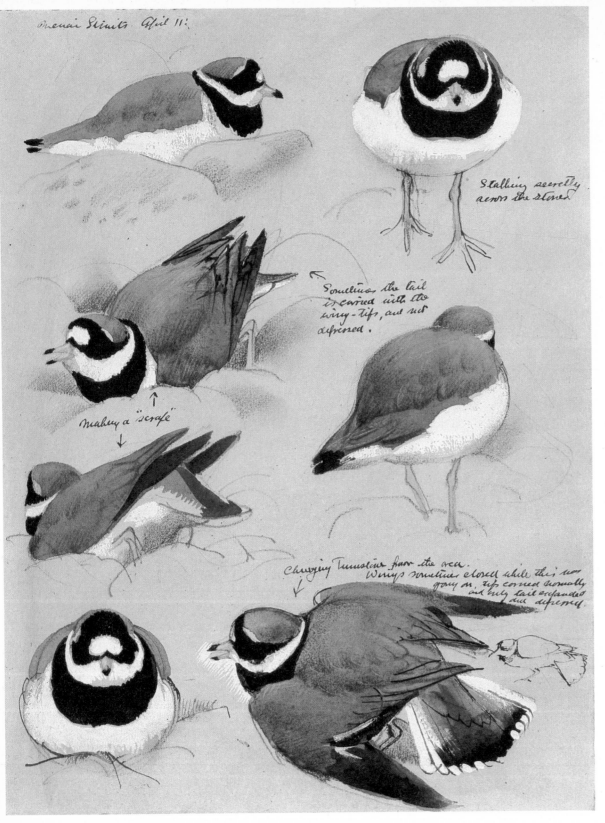

4 Ringed Plover *Charadrius hiaticula*, Menai Straits, April 11th 1954.

Another sheet of studio studies based on the field notes and sketches of courtship display reproduced on the previous pages.

Stalking secretly across the stones.

Sometimes the tail is carried with the wing-tips, and not depressed.

Chivvying Turnstone from the area. Wings sometimes closed while this was going on, tips carried normally and only tail expanded and depressed.

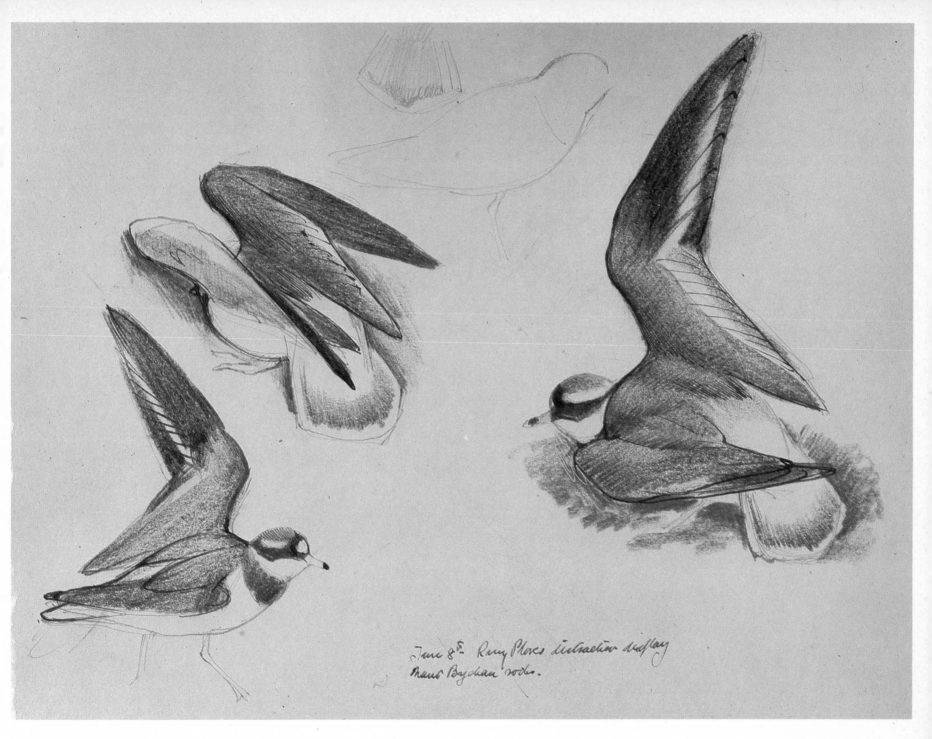

5 Ringed Plover *Charadrius hiaticula*, Nant Bychan rocks, June 8th 1949.

The Ringed Plover was performing its distraction display, the "broken wing trick", in the hope of luring the artist away from its eggs or chicks.

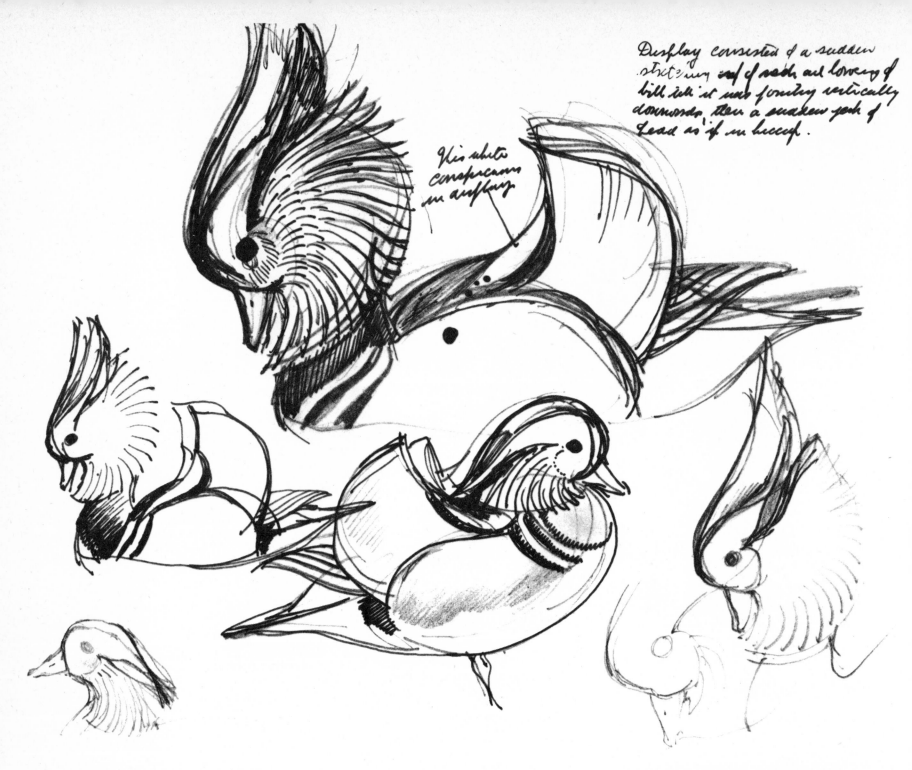

Display consisted of a sudden stretching up of neck and lowering of bill till it was pointing vertically downwards, then a sudden jerk of head as if in hiccup.

This white conspicuous in display

6 and **7** Mandarin *Aix galericulata*, Slimbridge, May 13th (? year).

Field pencil sketches, and the resulting worked-up studio drawing of the courtship displays of Mandarin. From a sketchbook containing drawings made during a visit to the Wildfowl Trust.

Display consisted of a sudden stretching up of neck and lowering of bill till it was pointing vertically downwards, then a sudden jerk of head as if in hiccup.

Mandarin drakes displaying by a female. Neck up, bill down, head decorations expanded. Orange wing feathers raised. Sudden jerky movements of head up and down.

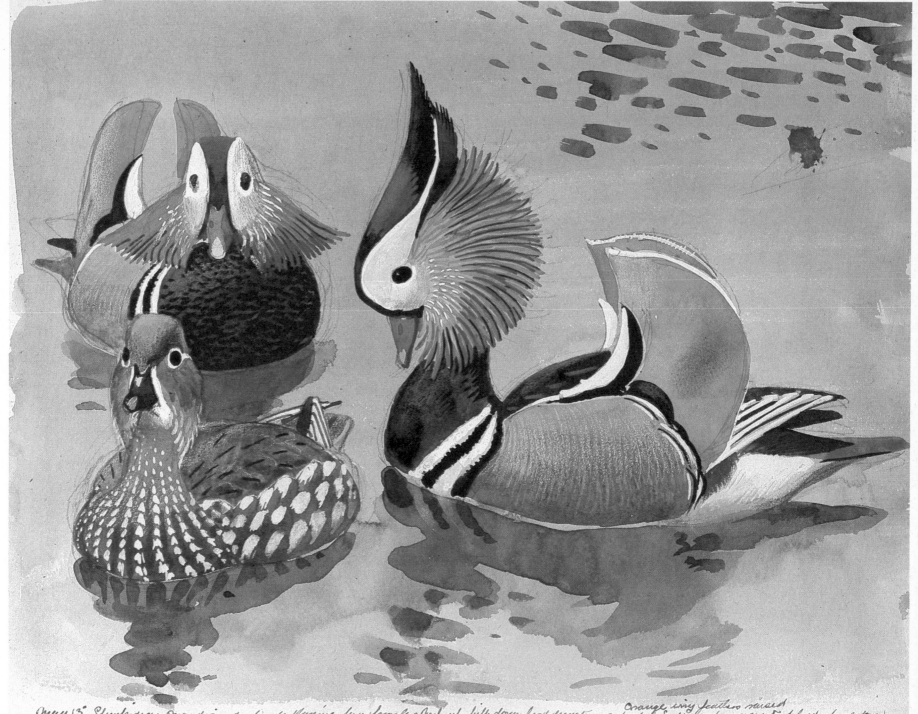

May 13ᵗʰ Slimbridge. Mandarin drakes displaying to a female. Neck up, bill down, head decorations expanded. Orange wing feathers raised. Sudden jerky movements of head up and down

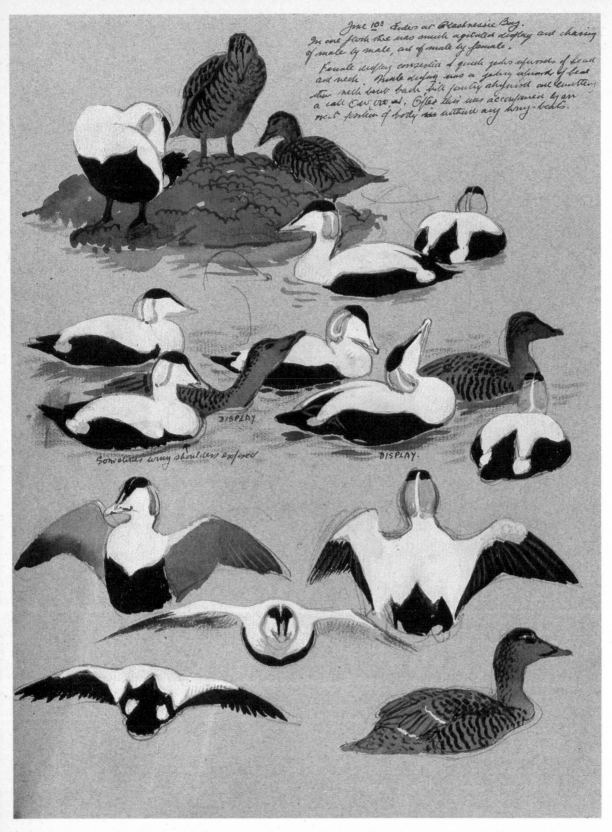

June 10th Eiders at Glashnessie Bay.
In one flock there was much agitated display and chasing
of male by male, and of male by female.

Female display consisted of quick jerks upwards of head
and neck. Male display was a jerking upward of head
then neck bent back, bill pointing skyward and emitting
a call Ow oo. Often this was accompanied by an
erect position of body without any wing-beats.

Sometimes wing shoulders exposed

DISPLAY

DISPLAY.

8 Eider *Somateria mollissima*, Glashnessie Bay, June 10th 1953.

In one flock there was much agitated display and chasing of male by male, and male by female. Female display consisted of quick jerks upwards of head and neck. Male display was a jerking upward of head then neck bent back, bill pointing skyward and emitting a call Ow oo. Often this was accompanied by an erect position of body without any wing-beats.

9 Goldeneye *Bucephala clangula*, Shorelands, February 27th 1956.

A bitterly cold morning with a thawing wind. Small flock of Goldeneye on the river in front of the studio. Much excitement among them. There were at least six adult drakes in a flock of 13 or 14. Many times 3 or 4 drakes would go into display contortions in front of, or near, one duck. In the backward bending of neck position a jet of water was sometimes kicked up, but not always.

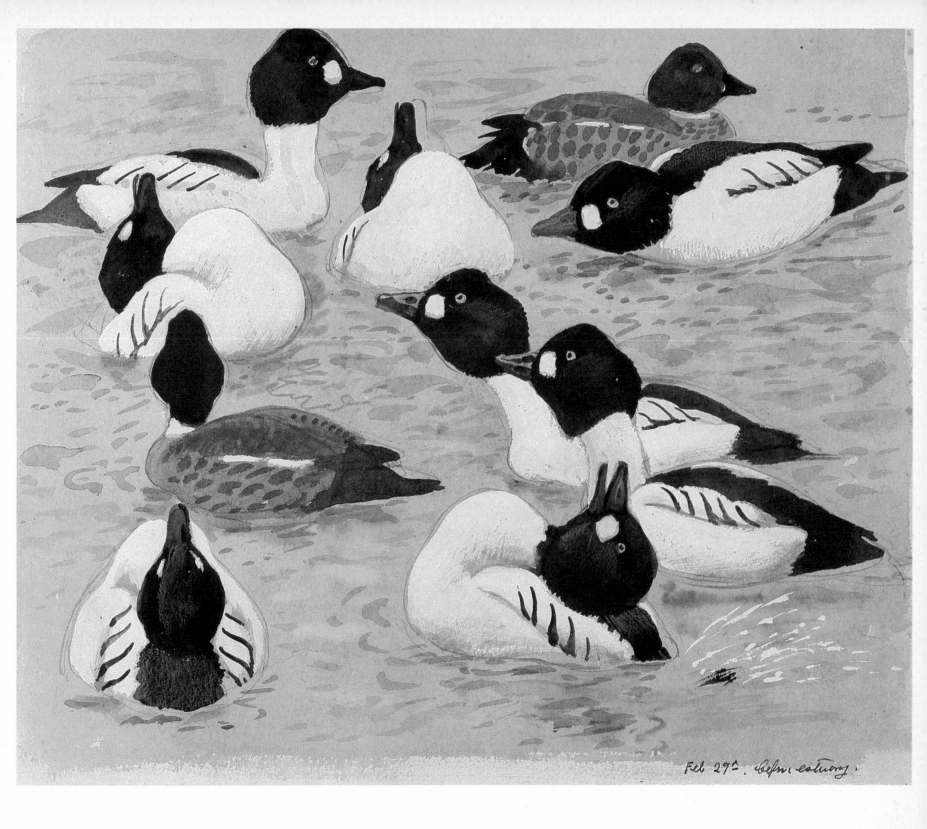

Feb 27. Cefni estuary.

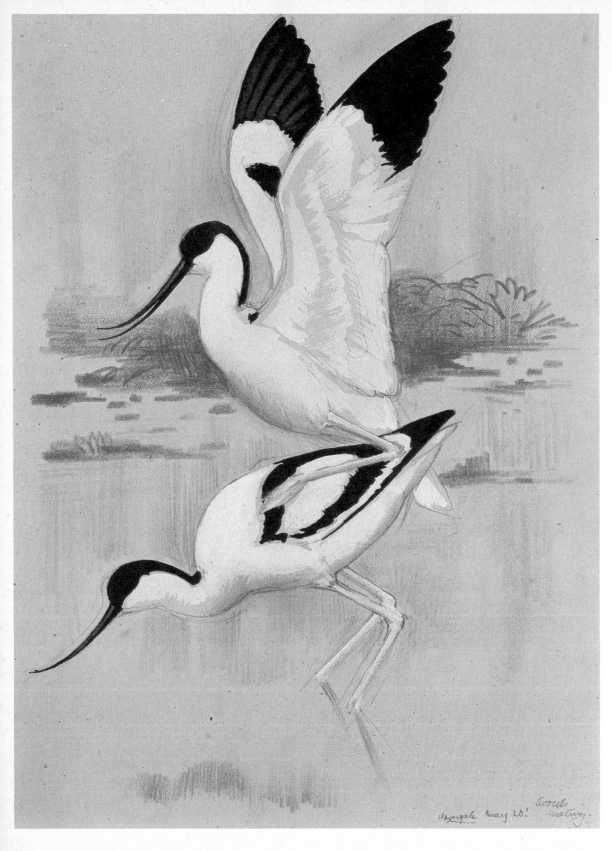

10 Avocet *Recurvirostra avosetta*, Havergate Island, May 20th 1950.

A pair of Avocets mating.

The return of Avocets to breed in East Anglia in 1947, and their subsequent protection and management by the R.S.P.B., is one of the great post war success stories of conservation. In 1950 it was decided to lift the veil of secrecy and the R.S.P.B., as well as allowing the birds to be photographed, invited Tunnicliffe to make a series of drawings for their booklet *Avocets in England* which was published later that year. His Suffolk sketchbook contains drawings of a number of the rarer species which nested on the R.S.P.B. reserves at Minsmere and Havergate, and Tunnicliffe used these later when making paintings for the Society's Christmas cards and journal covers.

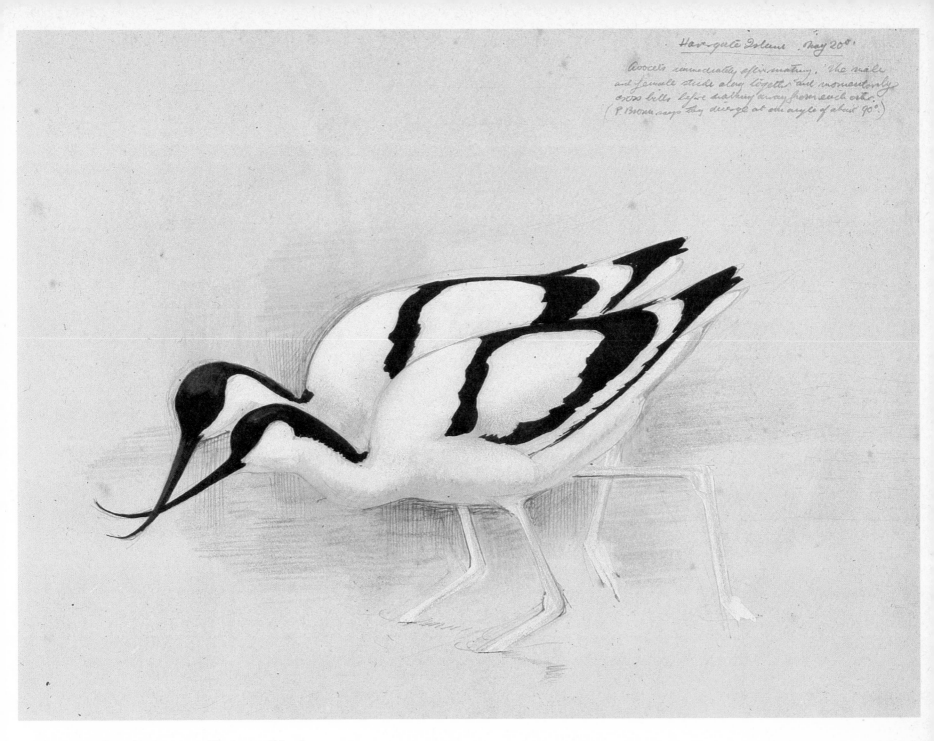

Havergate Island. May 20th.

Avocets immediately after mating. The male and female stride along together and momentarily cross bills before walking away from each other. (P. Brown says they diverge at an angle of about 90°.)

11 Avocet *Recurvirostra avosetta*, Havergate Island, May 20th 1950.

Avocets immediately after mating. The male and female stride along together and momentarily cross bills before walking away from each other. (P. Brown says they diverge at an angle of about 90°.)

usual carriage of body when walking.
Sometimes body is held higher at shoulders
and lower at tail

12 and **13** Avocet *Recurvirostra avosetta*, Havergate Island, May 1950.

Further studies of Avocets, walking, flying and alighting. Tunnicliffe frequently added notes to his sketches to remind himself of details of bird behaviour.

Usual carriage of body when walking. Sometimes body is held higher at shoulders and lower at tail.

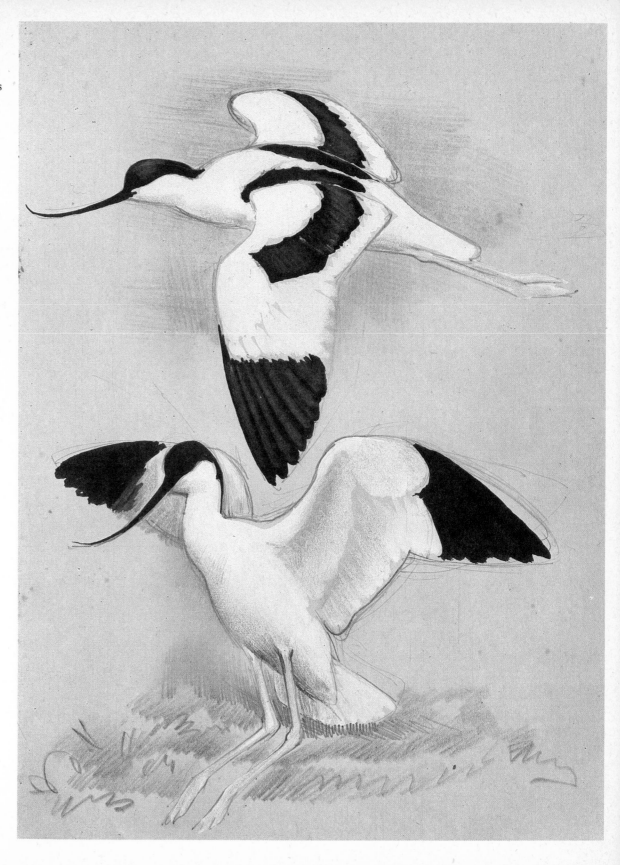

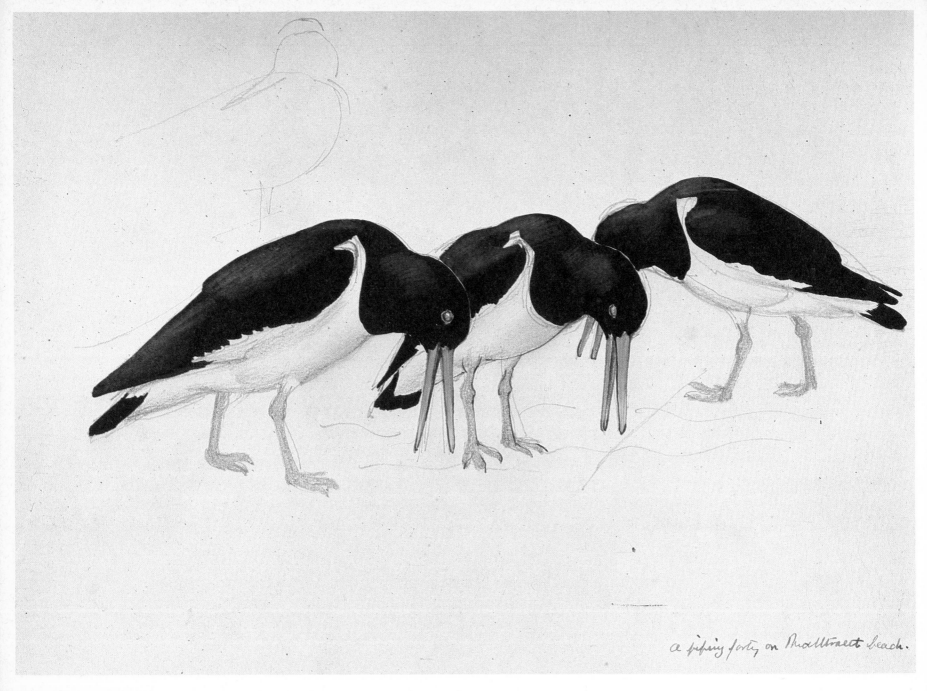

a piping party on Malltraeth beach.

14 Oystercatcher *Haematopus ostralegus*, Malltraeth beach, May 1944.

A piping ceremony of Oystercatchers consists of a small group, excitedly running along with bills pointing down and calling loudly. The exact function of this noisy behaviour is not clear but it occurs during courtship and territorial encounters.

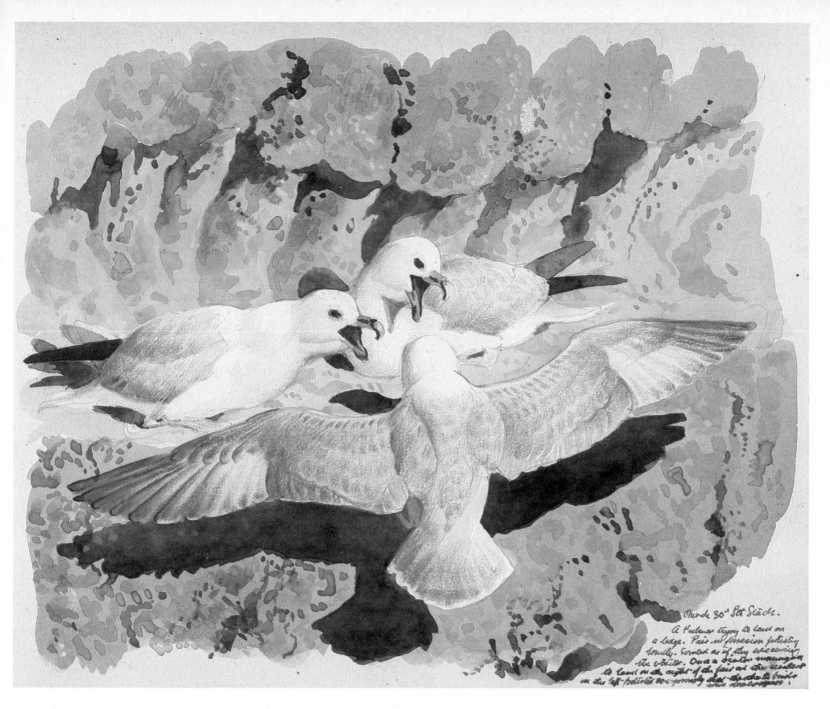

15 Fulmar *Fulmarus glacialis*, South Stack, March 30th 1951.

A Fulmar trying to land on a ledge. Pair in possession protesting loudly. Sounded as if they were cursing the visitor. Once a visitor managed to land on the right of the pair and the nearest on the left protested so vigorously that the other 2 birds were dislodged.

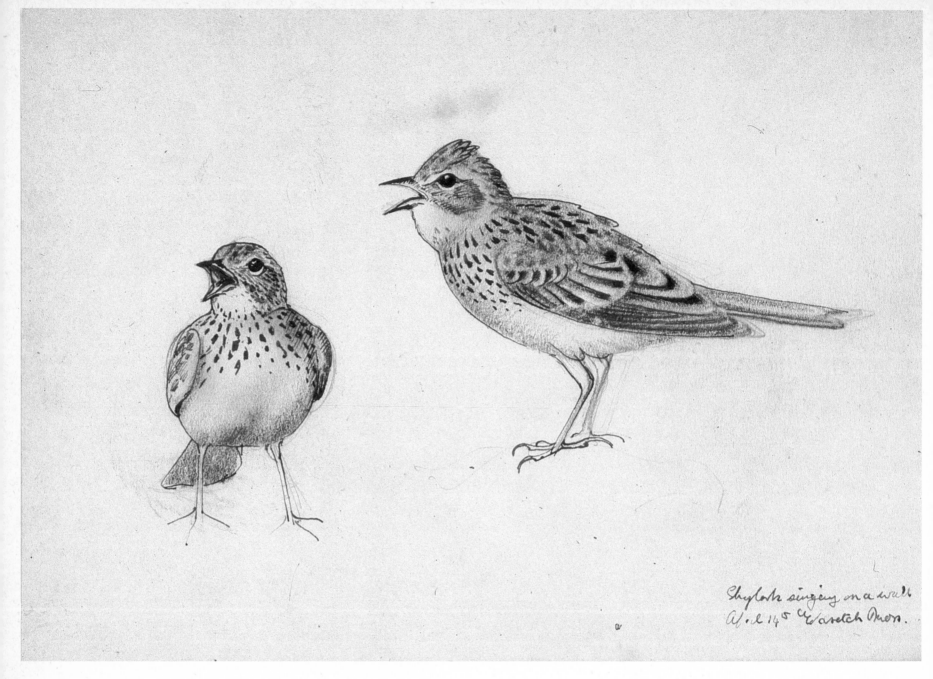

Skylark singing on a wall
April 14ᵗʰ Wavetch Moss.

16 Skylark *Alauda arvensis*, Goldsitch Moss, April 14th 1947.

A bird singing on a wall.

The young bird

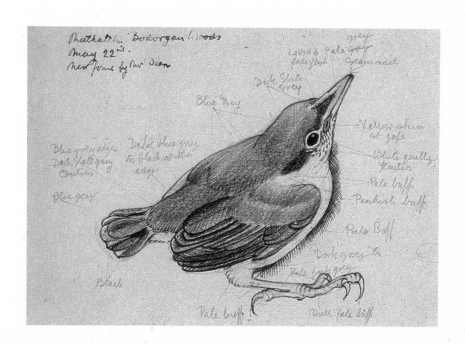

The theme of adults and young, the family, is constantly present in Tunnicliffe's work. The families that were so familiar around his home in Anglesey—parties of Shelducklings with their protective parents, the young Peregrines growing daily stronger at the cliff eyrie, the many seabird colonies and the family groups of waders and gulls which came to the shore outside his studio window—these are the scenes which fill the summer pages of the sketchbooks and are used later as subjects for paintings and illustrations. Watching the behaviour of adults and young has endless fascination: the tiresome young Black-headed Gulls (**32**) or Oystercatcher (**36**), trying to persuade their parents to provide food for them. The Green Woodpecker which fed its youngster outside the studio (**37**) gave Tunnicliffe an excellent view of exactly how the young bird begged and how the adult regurgitated the ants it had been finding; his notes are a model of succinct information.

This section includes a group of drawings made at the R.S.P.B. heath and marshland reserve at Minsmere in Suffolk. It was here that Tunnicliffe met Eric Hosking, the great bird photographer, and asked his advice about a Bittern he was painting and which he felt was not quite right. Eric Hosking recalls the occasion in his autobiography *An Eye for a Bird*. "I said that the position of the eye was inaccurate. He had used the skin of a bittern as a basis for his sketches and this, of course, did not show the eyes which are not right on the sides of its head but slightly forward of that position—the bird is a trifle boss-eyed. As I had a hide at a bittern's nest I suggested to Charles that he should use it. When I returned for him a couple of hours later he was as excited as a schoolboy. Never before had he seen a bittern at such close range."

The results of Tunnicliffe's sojourn in Hosking's hide are illustrated here—numbers **26–29**. He went on to work from twelve other hides at nests of Stone Curlew, Bearded Tit, Woodlark and others. Tunnicliffe was, in Hosking's word, *thrilled* to have the opportunity to sketch scarce species at close quarters. His few weeks in Suffolk produced a series of memorable drawings, some of which he used later for R.S.P.B. publications.

The nestling Carrion Crows (**18**) and Shags (**19**) are from a sketchbook full of drawings made on or around Skomer Island, off the Pembrokeshire coast, in 1949, when Tunnicliffe was at the height of his powers as an artist.

The young Oystercatcher (**36**), "attempting to coax food from its parent", was drawn at Nant Bychan rocks at the beginning of September and used in *Shorelands Summer Diary* to illustrate similar behaviour seen on the shore in front of the house on August 10th. Careful annotation of field sketches is essential for all wildlife artists. Tunnicliffe was a meticulous ornithologist and never used his material out of context.

Previous page: Nuthatch *Sitta europaea*

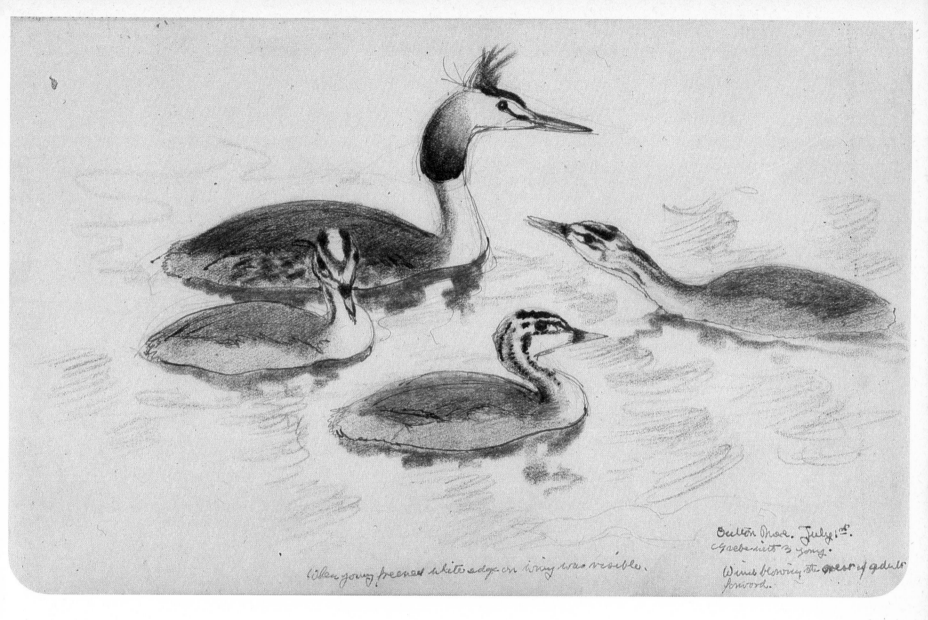

When young preened white edge on wing was visible.

Oulton Mere. July 1st.
Grebe with 3 young.
Wind blowing the crest of adult
forward.

17 Great Crested Grebe *Podiceps cristatus*, Oulton Mere, July 1st 1939.

However, a Great Crested Grebe with three young provided ample compensation. When I came into view the three young-birds dived at once but not so the parent. She watched me intently, her crest blown forwards over her crown. I sat down on the bank, and presently the group composed itself. The youngsters were well grown and had lost the stripes on the front of their breasts, but on their heads and necks the stripes were still quite distinct. Their bills were pink with a black band near their base. Their grey backs and brown-grey flanks were well fledged, and. as they preened I caught a glimpse of white wing feathers. At intervals they went to their mother with outstretched necks and open mouths calling shrilly for food. They looked most reptilian in this attitude. She sometimes obliged, diving and soon reappearing with a small fish which was at once taken by one of the young.

Mereside Chronicle

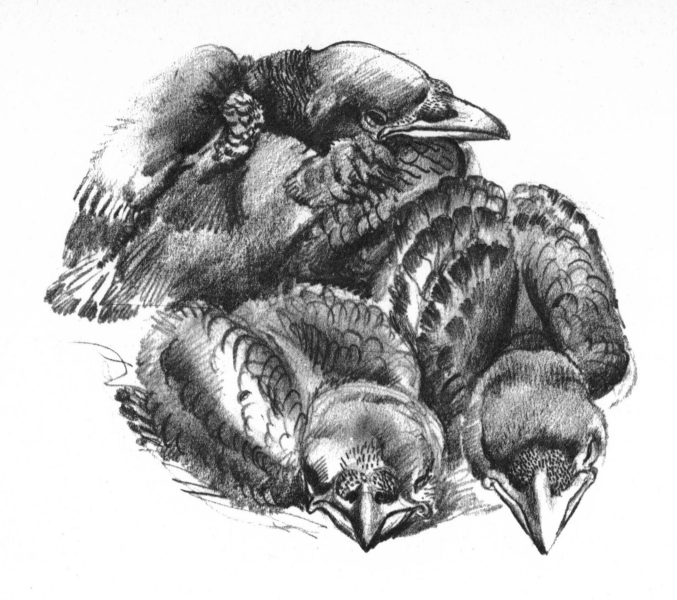

18 Carrion Crow *Corvus corone*, Skomer Island,
May 24th 1949.

Partly fledged young in a nest on a rock pile.

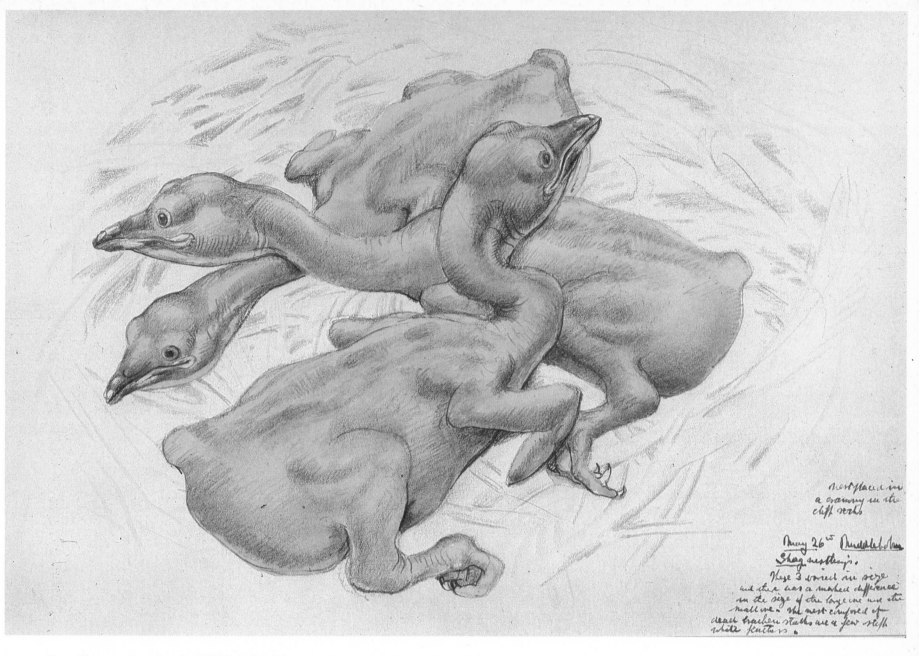

Nest placed in
a cranny in the
cliff rocks

May 26th Middleholm
Shag nestlings.
These 3 varied in size
and there was a marked difference
in the size of the large one and the
small one. The nest composed of
dead bracken stalks and a few stiff
white feathers.

19· Shag *Phalacrocorax aristotelis*, Middleholm, May
26th 1949.

*These 3 varied in size and there was a marked difference
in the size of the large one and the small one. The nest
composed of dead bracken stalks and a few stiff white
feathers. Nest placed in a cranny in the cliff rocks.*

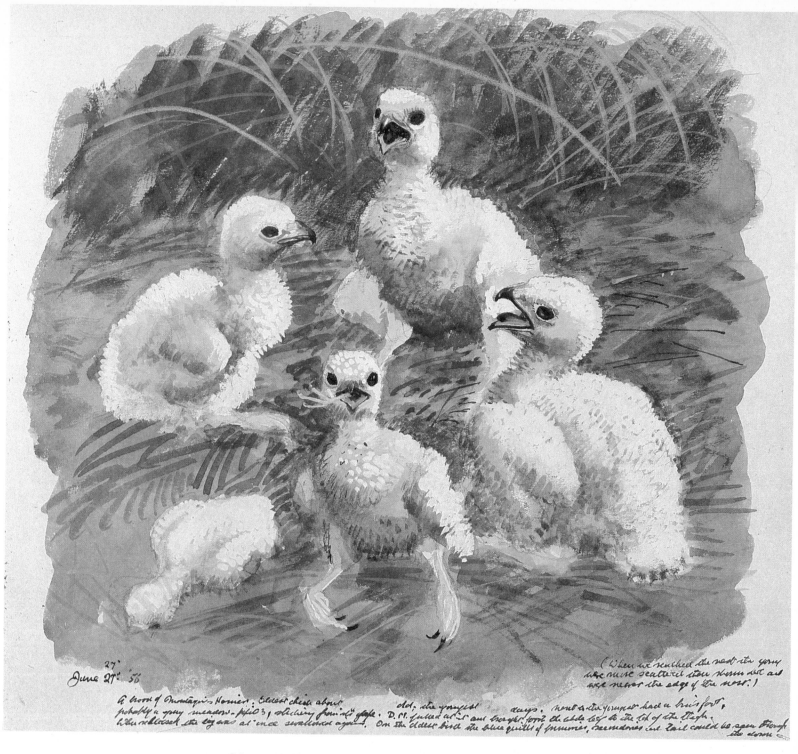

A brood of Montagu's Harriers. Oldest chick about 8 days old, the youngest 4 days. Next to the youngest had a bird's foot, probably a young Meadow Pipit's, sticking from its gape. D.M. pulled at it and brought forth the whole leg to the top of the thigh. When released the leg was at once swallowed again. On the older bird the blue quills of primaries, secondaries and tail could be seen through the down. (When we reached the nest the young were more scattered than shown here and were nearer the edge of the nest.)

20 Montagu's Harrier *Circus pygargus*, Anglesey, June 27th 1956.

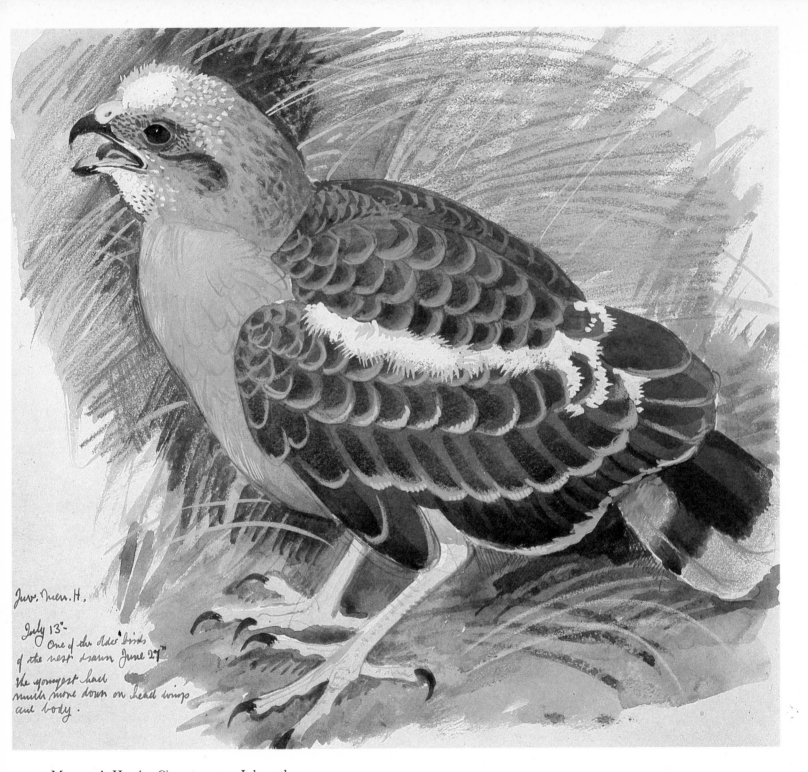

Juv. Mon. H.

July 13ᵗ⁻
One of the older birds
of the nest drawn June 27ᵗʰ
the youngest had
much more down on head wings
and body.

21 Montagu's Harrier *Circus pygargus*, July 13th
1956.

Juvenile, about four weeks old.

*One of the older birds of the nest drawn June 27th. The
youngest had much more down on head, wings and body.*

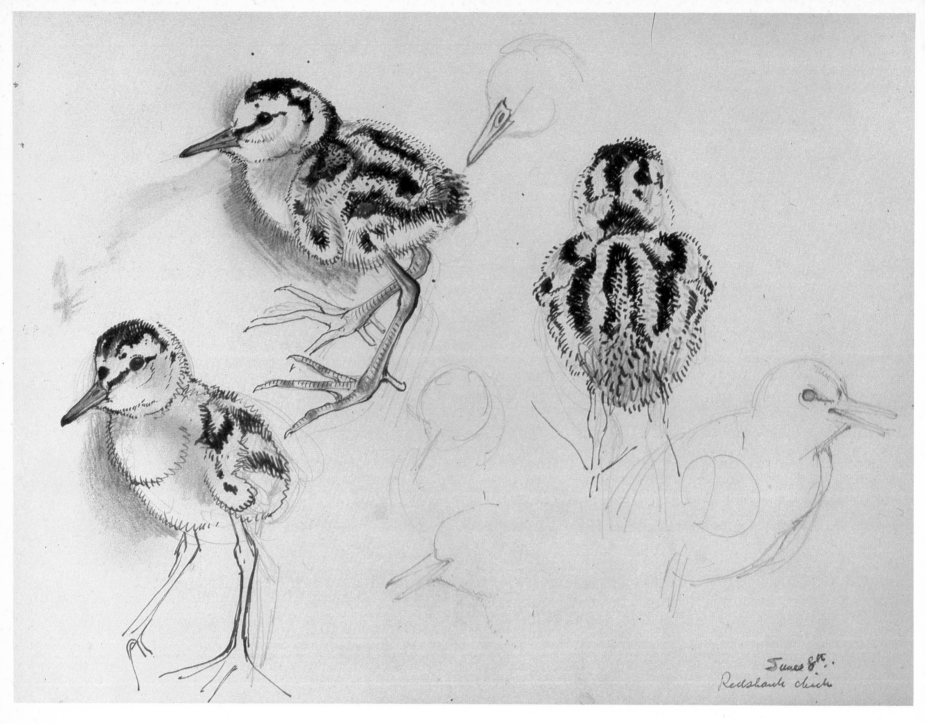

22 Redshank *Tringa totanus*, Anglesey, June 8th 1949.

The sketches on these two pages were drawn in a mixture of pencil, pen and ink, coloured crayon and a small amount of opaque wash.

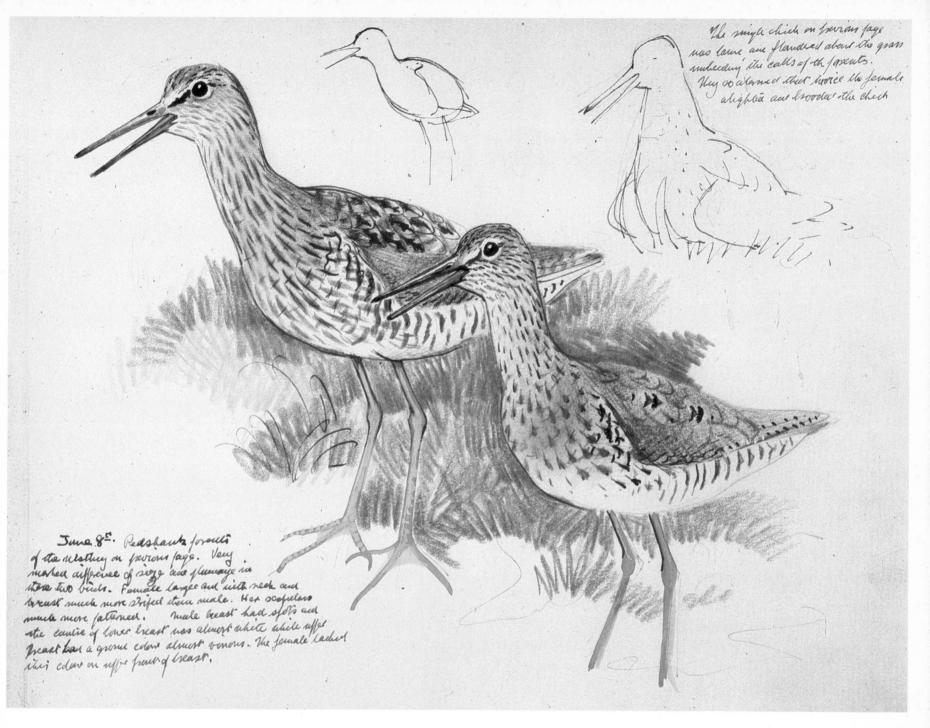

The single chick on previous page was lame and floundered about the grass unheeding the calls of the parents. They so alarmed that twice the female alighted and brooded the chick.

June 8th. Redshank parents of the nestling on previous page. Very marked difference of size and plumage in these two birds. Female larger and with neck and breast much more striped than male. Her scapulars much more patterned. Male breast had spots and the centre of lower breast was almost white while upper breast had a ground colour almost vinous. The female lacked this colour on upper front of breast.

23 Redshank *Tringa totanus*, Anglesey, June 8th 1949.

Redshank parents of the nestling on previous page. Very marked difference of size and plumage in these two birds. Female larger and with neck and breast much more striped than male. Her scapulars much more patterned. Male breast had spots and the centre of lower breast was almost white while upper breast had a ground colour almost vinous. The female lacked this colour on upper front of breast.

The single chick on previous page was lame and floundered about the grass unheeding the calls of the parents. They so alarmed that twice the female alighted and brooded the chick.

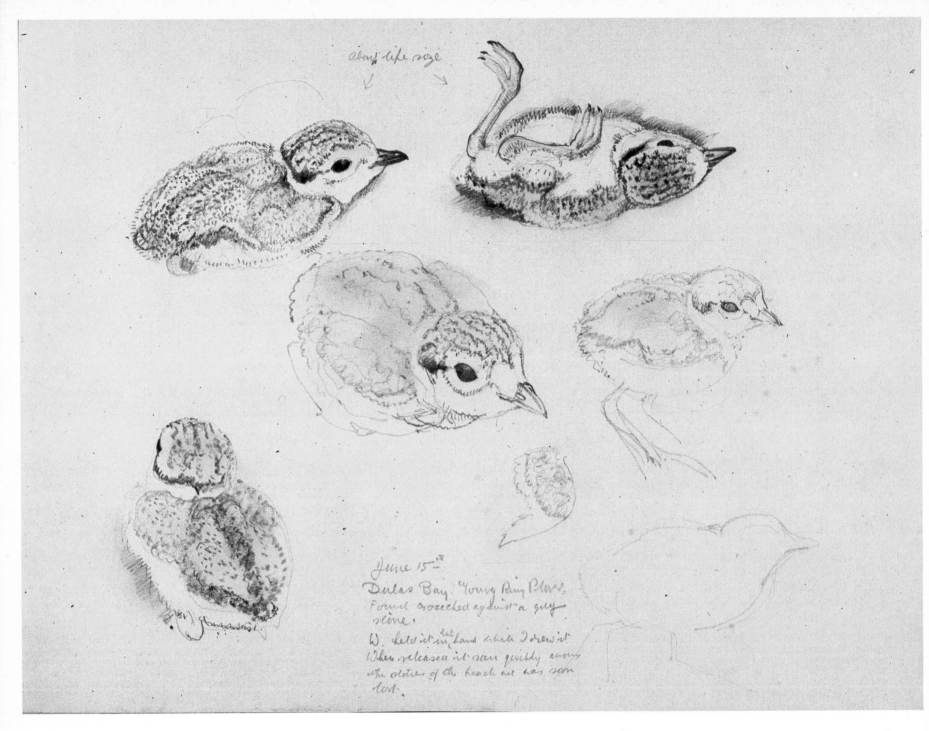

24 Ringed Plover *Charadrius hiaticula*, Dulas Bay, June 15th 1948.

Later I saw the chicks again, nearer the sea this time and in easier terrain of sand and boulders. So I made a second dash and, after a short search, came upon a chick crouching against a grey stone. The chick seemed to be the offspring of the stone itself, mottled grey against mottled grey. I picked it up and it was in no way perturbed, but lay in my hand quietly. I gave it to W. who held it while I made a drawing. It crouched on her palm and did not move. Then as I wanted the underside of the chick W. turned it over and it lay quietly on its back with legs in the air until I had completed another drawing.

Shorelands Summer Diary.

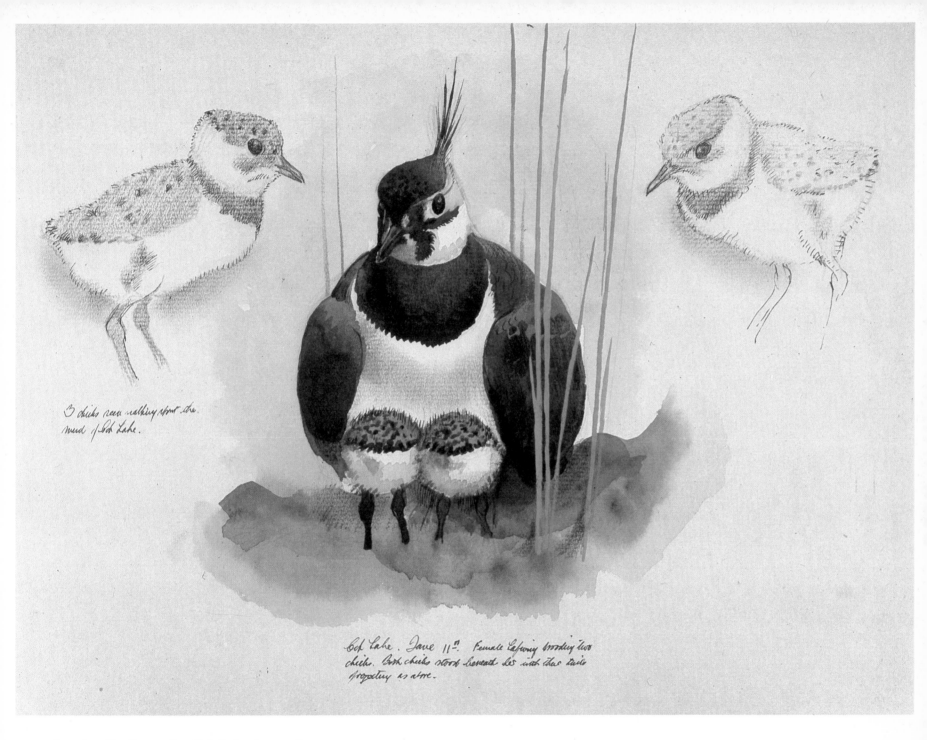

3 chicks seen walking about the mud of Cob Lake.

Cob Lake. June 11th. Female Lapwing brooding two chicks. Both chicks stood beneath her with their tails projecting as above.

25 Lapwing *Vanellus vanellus*, Cob Lake, June 11th
1970.

Female Lapwing brooding two chicks.

*Both chicks stood beneath her with their tails projecting as
above.*

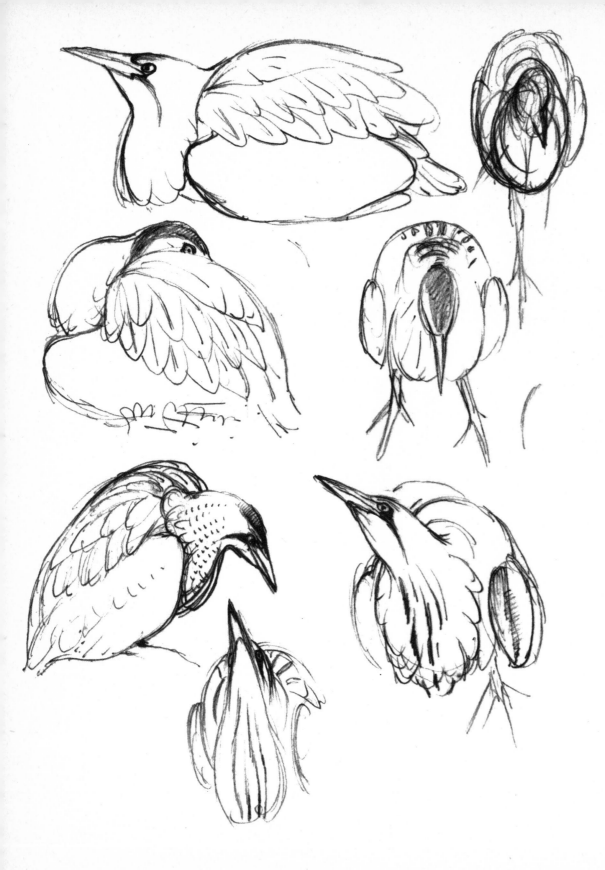

26 Bittern *Botaurus stellaris*, Minsmere, May 30th 1950.

Tunnicliffe worked from a hide when making these sketches of a Bittern at its nest, deep in a reed bed on the R.S.P.B. reserve at Minsmere in Suffolk.

27 Bittern *Botaurus stellaris*, Minsmere, May 30th 1950.

Bittern with 3 chicks and one egg chipping. When I went into the hide she did not return until forty mintues had elapsed. Then she stroked the egg and tried to get all the chicks under her but only partly succeeded. Often her neck would stretch out to reach a piece of reed and this she built into the nest side.

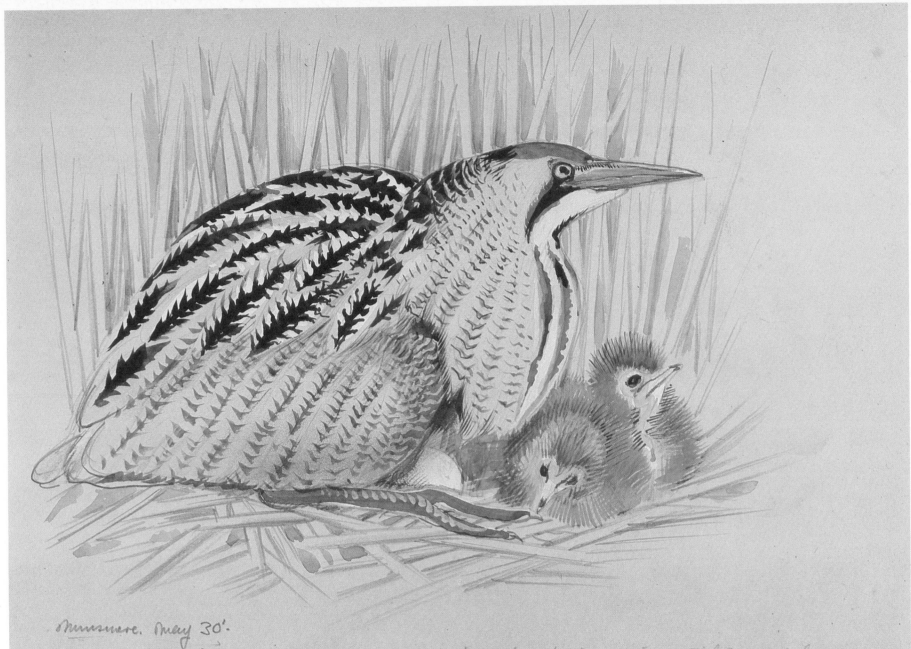

Minsmere. May 30'.

Bittern with 3 chicks and one egg chipping. When I went into the hide she did not return until forty minutes had elapsed. Then she shielded the egg and dead so that all the chicks were her but only partially succeeded. Often her neck would stretch out to reach a piece of reed and this she pushed into the nest side

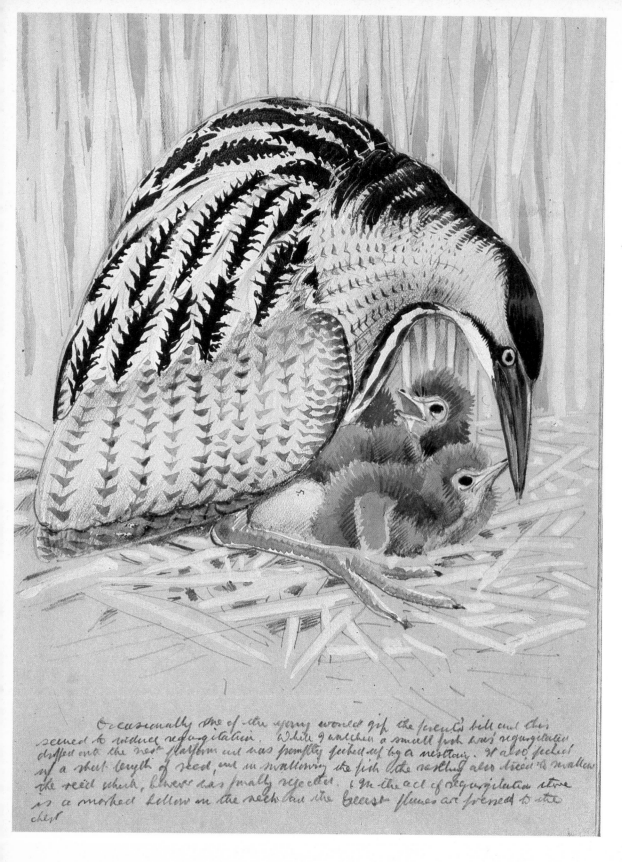

28 Bittern *Botaurus stellaris*, Minsmere, May 30th 1950.

Occasionally one of the young would grip the parent's bill and this seemed to induce regurgitation. While I watched a small fish was regurgitated, dropped onto the nest platform and was promptly picked up by a nestling. It also picked up a short length of reed, and on swallowing the fish the nestling also tried to swallow the reed which, however, was finally rejected. In the act of regurgitation there is a marked hollow in the neck and the breast plumes are pressed to the chest.

Occasionally one of the young would grip the parent's bill and this seemed to induce regurgitation. While I watched a small fish was regurgitated, dropped onto the nest platform and was promptly picked up by a nestling. It also picked up a short length of reed, and on swallowing the fish the nestling also tried to swallow the reed which, I believe, was finally rejected. In the act of regurgitation there is a marked hollow in the neck and the breast plumes are pressed to the chest.

29 Bearded Tit *Panurus biarmicus*, Minsmere, May 25th 1950.

Hen feeding young. Cock coming in with food.

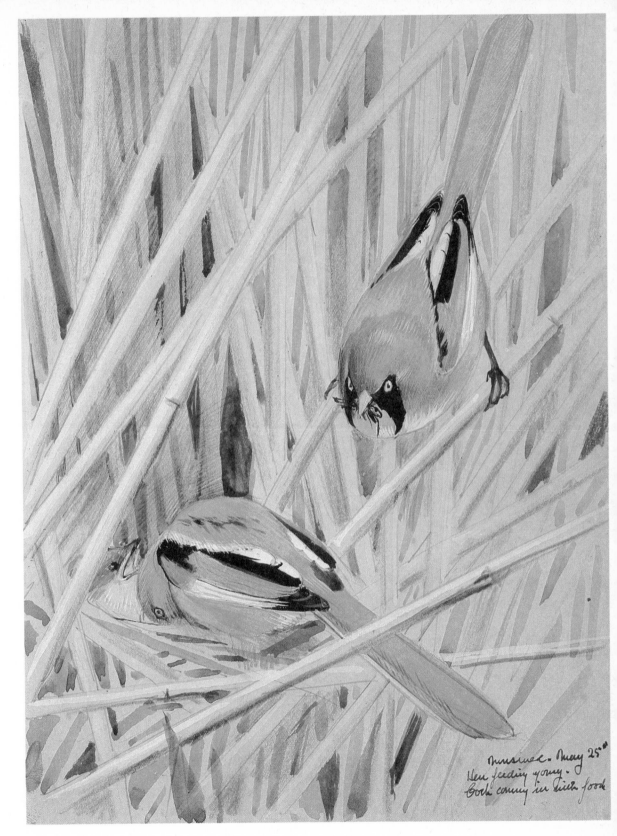

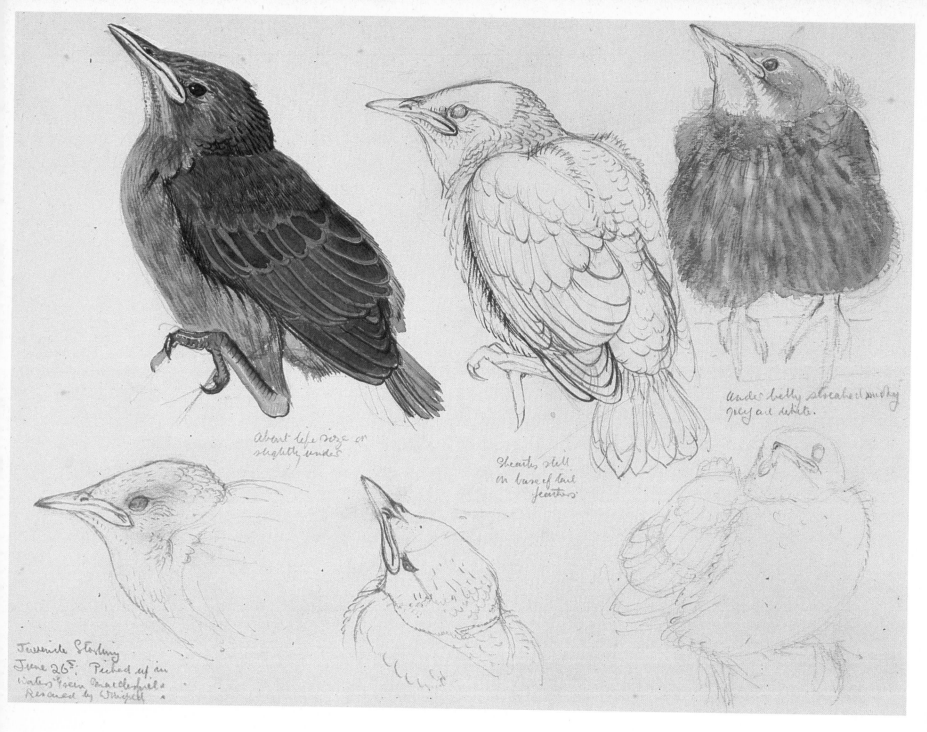

About life size or slightly under

Sheaths still on base of tail feathers

Under belly streaked smoky grey and white.

Juvenile Starling
June 26. Picked up in
Waters Green Macclesfield
Rescued by Winifred.

30 Starling *Sturnus vulgaris*, Macclesfield, June 26th 1945.

A fledgling Starling which had been picked up by Winifred Tunnicliffe in Waters Green, Macclesfield.

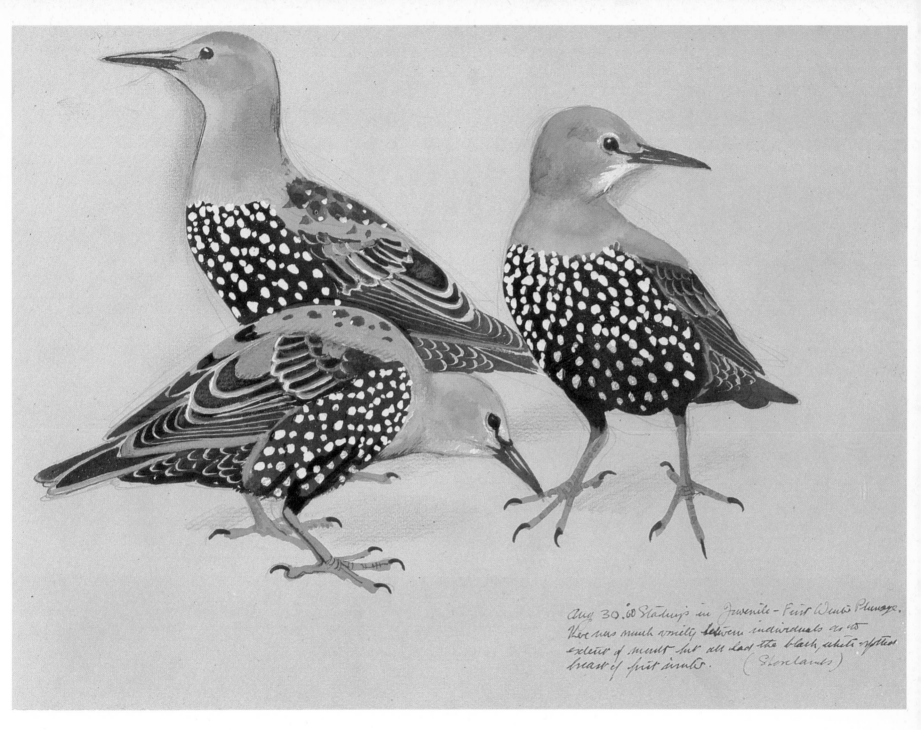

Aug 30. 60 Starlings in Juvenile-First Winter Plumage.
There was much variety between individuals as to
extent of moult but all had the black, white-spotted
breast of first winter. (Shorelands)

31 Starling *Sturnus vulgaris*, Shorelands, August
30th 1960.

*Starlings in Juvenile-First Winter Plumage. There was
much variety between individuals as to extent of moult but
all had the black, white-spotted breast of first winter.*

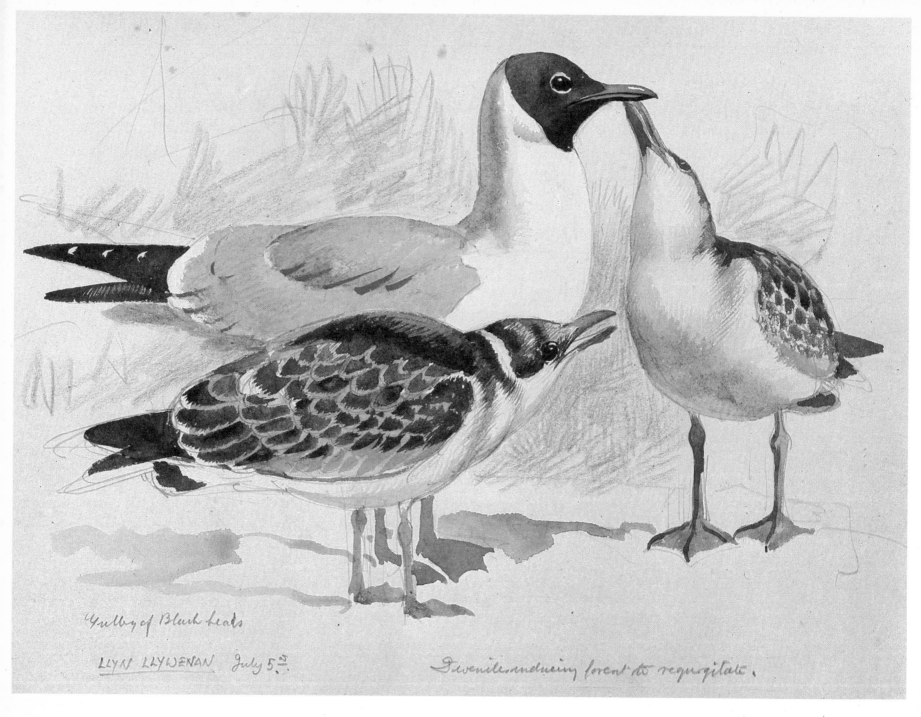

Gully of Black heads

LLYN LLYWENAN July 5th

Juveniles inducing parent to regurgitate.

32 Black-headed Gull *Larus ridibundus*, Llyn Llywenan, July 5th 1948.

Two young birds squeaked in front of an adult, their shoulders hunched and heads lowered, but for a time they were ignored. They approached nearer to their parent, one nuzzling her crop with its bill, while the other reached up and nibbled its parent's bill. This brought about the desired result for the parent bird seemed to gulp, then regurgitated a mass of something which the young birds eagerly swallowed. Again they asked for food and, again, they were successful, but, on pestering their parent a third time, it left the rock and settled on the water.

Shorelands Summer Diary.

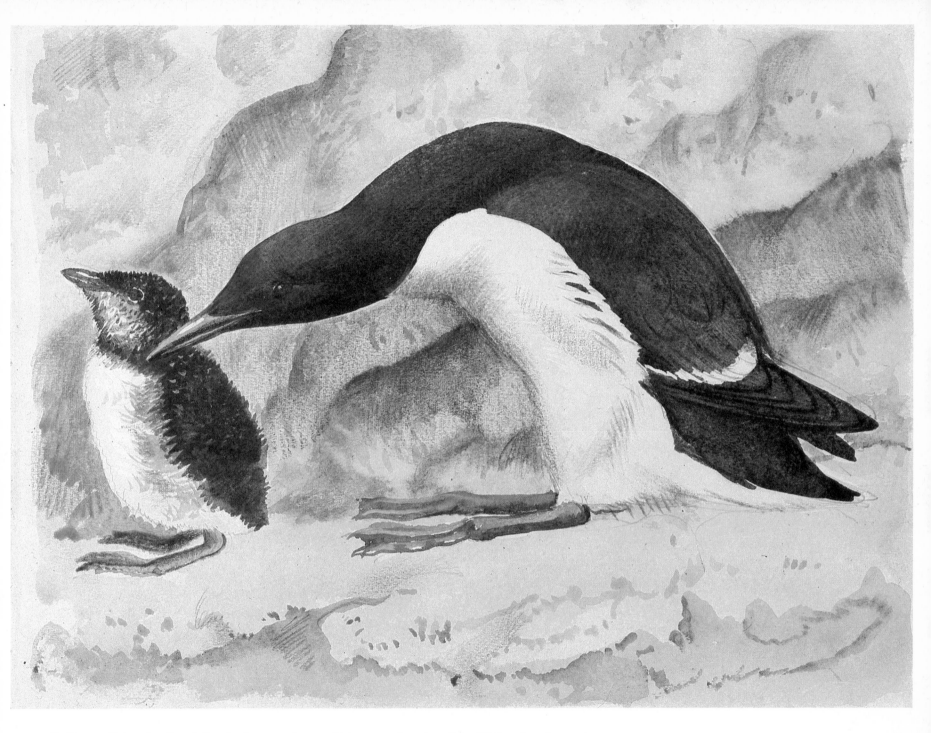

33 Guillemot *Uria aalge*, South Stack, August 7th 1948.

My new model, like the first, was preening, but it was much younger and more downy. Its parent was helping in its toilet, and was engrossed in nibbling and removing down from the infant, especially the down on neck and head. I made notes of this while sitting on a flat seat, *which commands a view of the cliff face through a crack in the rock. One of the lighthouse-keepers, at that moment coming up the steps, told me that I was highly honoured, for Queen Victoria had sat on that self-same slab. I could only reply that I hoped she found it more comfortable than did I!*

Shorelands Summer Diary.

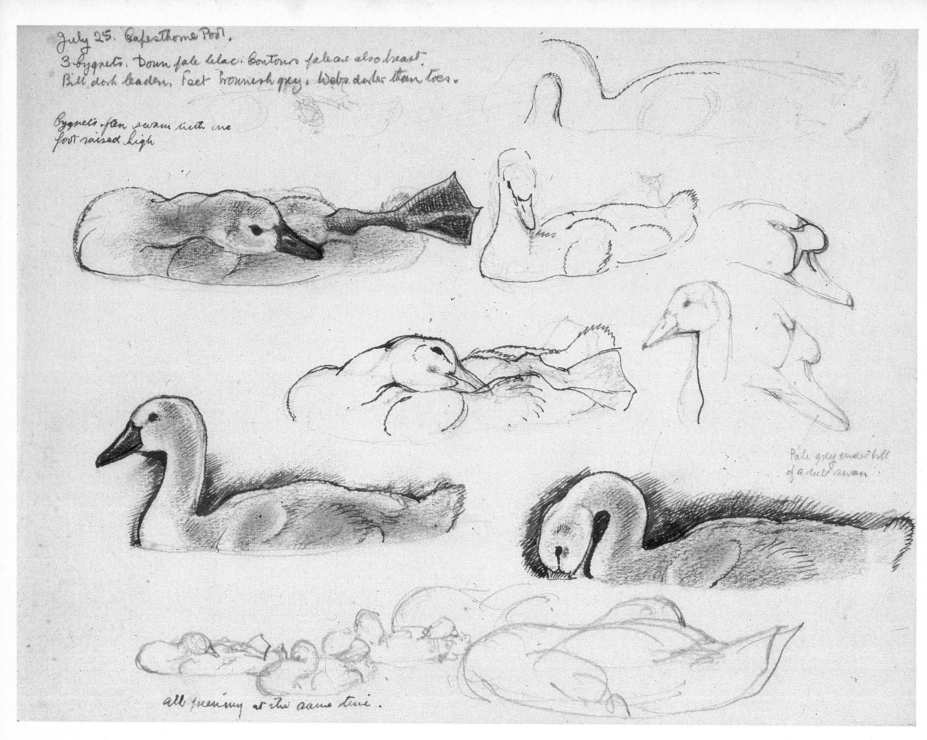

34 Mute Swan *Cygnus olor*, Capesthorne Pool, July 25th (? year).

3 cygnets. Down pale lilac. Contours pale and also breast. Bill dark leaden. Feet brownish grey. Webs darker than toes. Cygnets often swam with one foot raised high.

35 Shelduck *Tadorna tadorna*, Cob Lake, July 13th 1953.

Both parents in part eclipse, the female with a patch of white at base of bill and the chestnut band very diminished in width and obscured by white. While I watched all the young ran with wings flapping. Wings still undeveloped. Then all suddenly went to the grassy beach and as if at a signal squatted and began to preen. At the approach of either human or dog all take to the water.

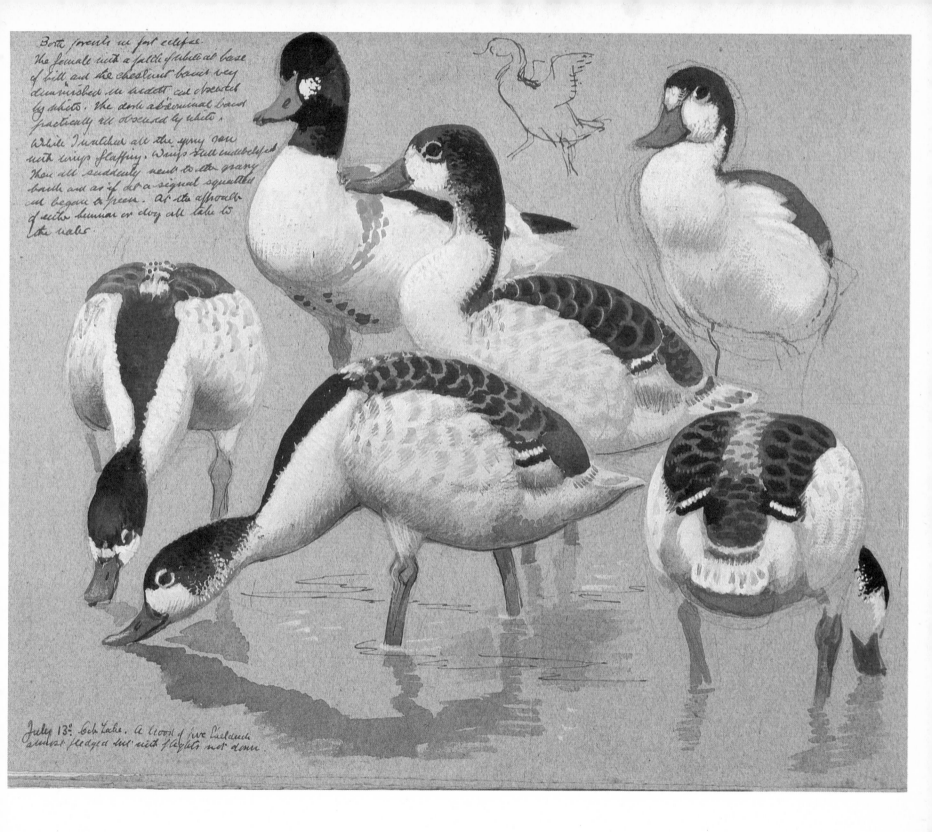

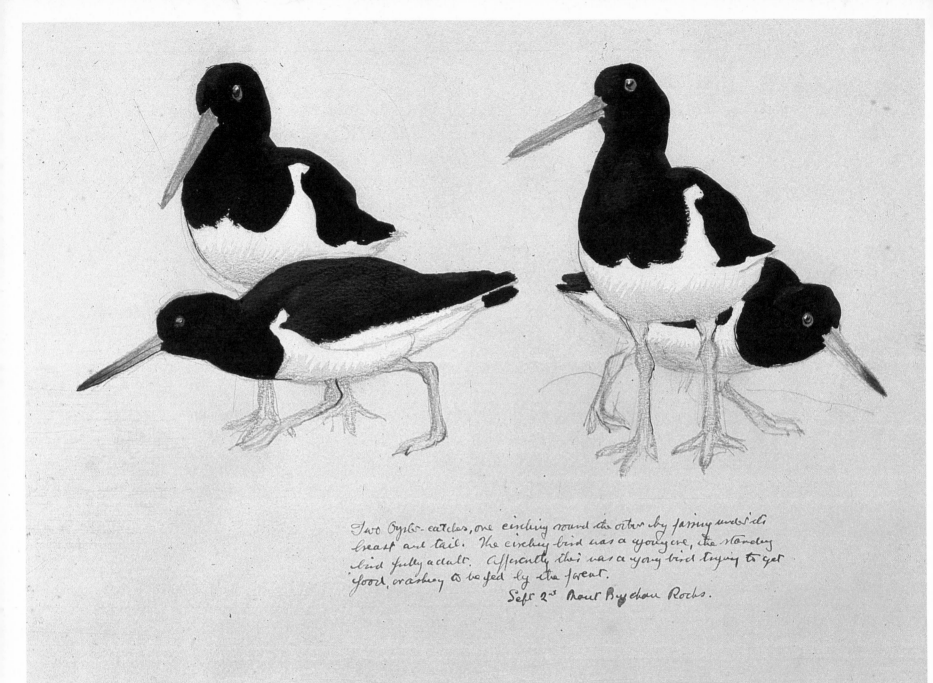

Two Oyster-catches, one circling round the other by passing under its breast and tail. The circling bird was a young one, the standing bird fully adult. Apparently this was a young bird trying to get food, or asking to be fed by the parent.
Sept 2nd Nant Bychan Rocks.

36 Oystercatcher *Haematopus ostralegus*, Nant Bychan rocks, September 2nd 1944.

This morning I watched a young Oystercatcher attempting to coax food from its parent. Both birds were on the sand in front of the house and I enjoyed a 'grandstand' view of the performance. The juvenile squeaked and whined by its parent's side and followed every move. When the old bird stood still the young one crouched and passed below its chest, repeating this manœuvre from one side to the other, and later, circling it completely, passed under the breast and tail of the parent, causing it to stand almost on tiptoe. Whenever the adult probed in the sand and found food the juvenile made a little rush to the same place; this indication of the whereabouts of food being all the help it received, it later decided to hunt for itself.

Shorelands Summer Diary.

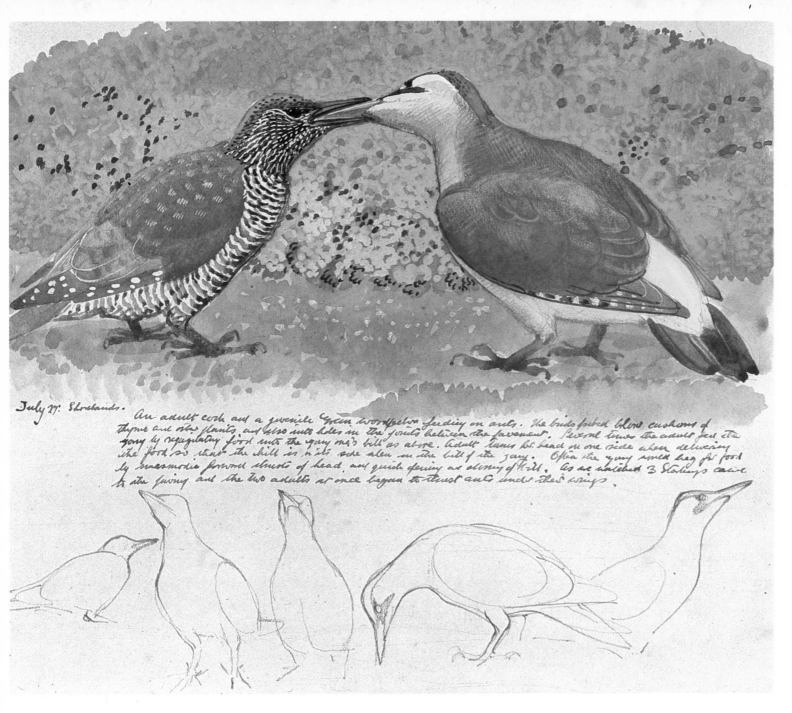

37 Green Woodpecker *Picus viridis*, Shorelands,
July 27th 1958.

*An adult cock and a juvenile Green Woodpecker feeding
on ants. The birds probed below cushions of thyme and
other plants and also into holes in the joints between the
pavement. Several times the adult fed the young by
regurgitating food into the young one's bill as above.
Adult turns his head on one side when delivering the food
so that the bill is on its side when in the bill of the young.
Often the young would beg for food by spasmodic forward
thrusts of head and quick opening and closing of bill. As
we watched 3 starlings came to the paving and the two
adults at once began to thrust ants under their wings.*

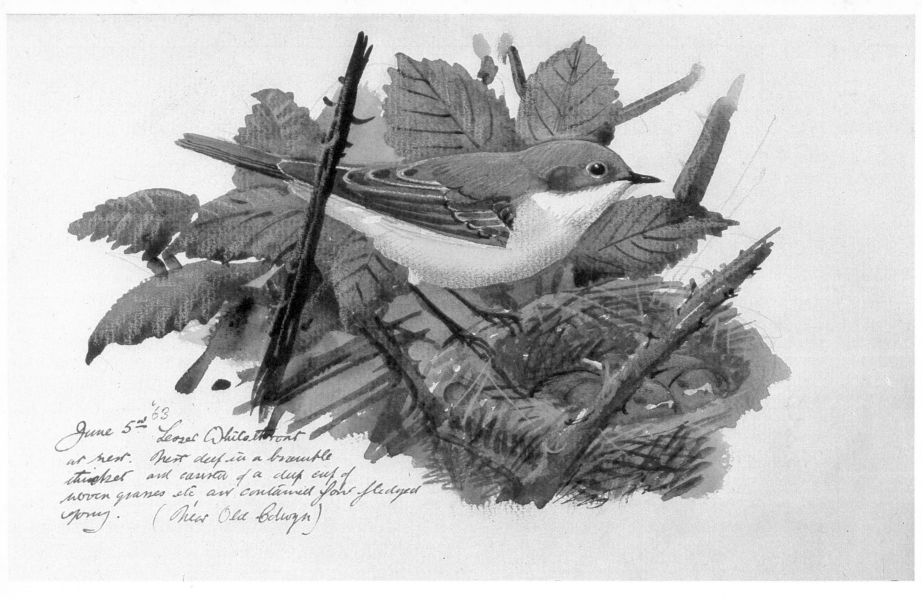

June 5th '63 Lesser Whitethroat
at nest. Nest deep in a bramble
thicket and consists of a deep cup of
woven grasses etc and contained four fledged
young. (Near Old Colwyn)

38 Lesser Whitethroat *Sylvia curruca*, Old Colwyn,
June 5th 1963.

*Nest deep in a bramble thicket and consisted of a deep cup
of woven grasses etc and contained four fledged young.*

Feeding

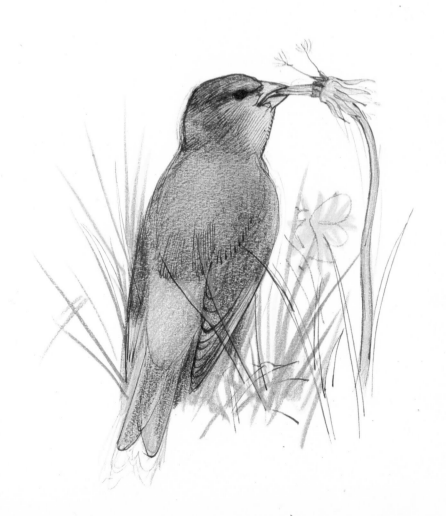

Birds spend the greater part of their waking hours in the search for food and the sketchbooks contain scores of drawings of birds absorbed in this vital activity. Most of these were not drawn for the express purpose of recording feeding behaviour; it was simply that Tunnicliffe sketched whatever the birds happened to be doing while he was watching. In many of these sketches, and their accompanying notes, Tunnicliffe has, however, recorded and described a number of different ways in which birds feed.

The area around Tunnicliffe's home on Anglesey, on the side of the Cefni estuary, was particularly good for wading birds and, judging by the sketchbooks, this was a group of birds in which he took a particular interest and greatly enjoyed drawing and painting. There are many ways in which waders seek their food. He records a Ringed Plover (**42**) patting the mud with one foot as it fed at the edge of Cob Lake. This foot trembling is almost confined to the plovers, only a few other waders having been seen doing it. It clearly helps in the capture of worms and other creatures but exactly how is still an open question. The two Greenshanks (**40**) watched feeding along the river edge opposite Tunnicliffe's house, fed with their bills flat on the top of the water, moving rapidly forward, evidently taking organisms from the surface as they went. Another Greenshank (**45**), was feeding belly-deep in water and repeatedly plunged its whole foreparts below the surface,

sometimes kicking with alternate strokes of the legs. This one was obviously finding quite different prey. Avocets have a typical feeding action of sweeping their long up-curved bills from side to side. Tunnicliffe made a particular note that two Avocets (**43**), which visited Cob Lake one March, were feeding with a regular prodding action in the mud—quite different from the more usual side to side sweeping motion.

The Curlew (**41**), walking at a leisurely pace and quietly probing the mud with its long, down-curved and very sensitive bill, appears to have a simple way of feeding. In fact the process is highly complex. The bird looks for visual clues on the mud—small holes or depressions, castings, movements below the surface—and it may also be listening for the slight sounds that large worms make as they burrow in the mud.

Tunnicliffe's sketchbooks contain a tremendous variety of observations and records of what he saw on his frequent, and at times daily, field trips. He records the sightings of unusual species, the unexpected behaviour of common species and the occasional avian dramas that any regular field observer will witness. His observations are all the more interesting for his descriptive powers with words as well as pencil, and his remarkable visual memory. He occasionally recorded a whole sequence of actions, annotated in detail, such as the fascinating account of the actions of a pair of Peregrines when they found a Redshank (**58** and **59**) which had been shot.

Previous page: Greenfinch *Chloris chloris*

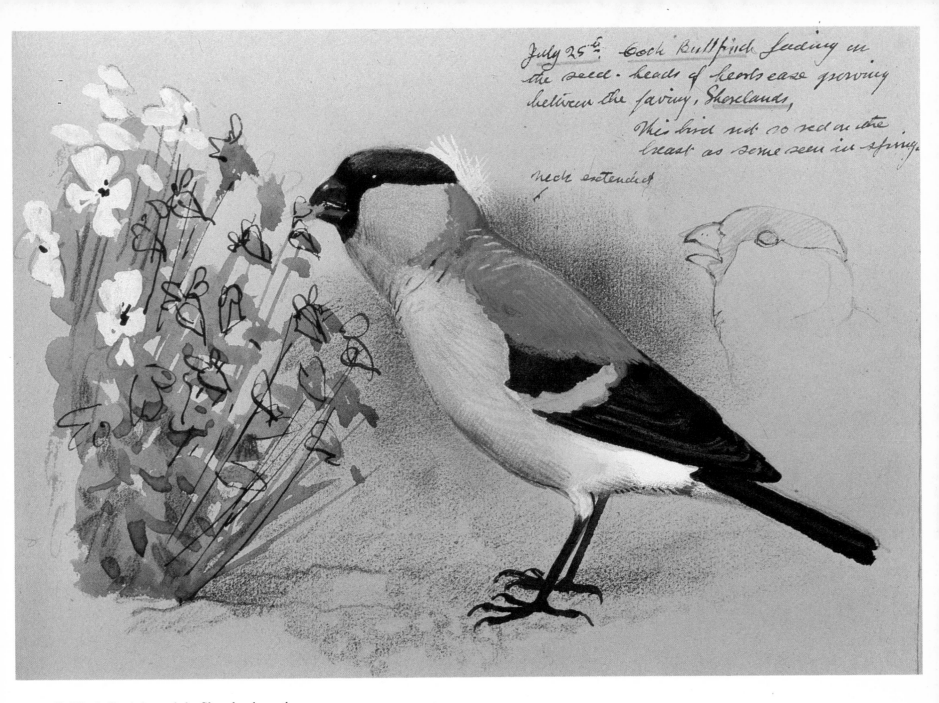

July 25ᵗʰ Cock Bullfinch feeding on the seed-heads of hearts ease growing between the paving, Shorelands.

This bird not so red on the breast as some seen in spring.

neck extended

39 Bullfinch *Pyrrhula pyrrhula*, Shorelands, 25th July 1954.

Cock Bullfinch feeding on the seed-heads of Hearts Ease growing between the paving, Shorelands. This bird not so red on the breast as some seen in spring.

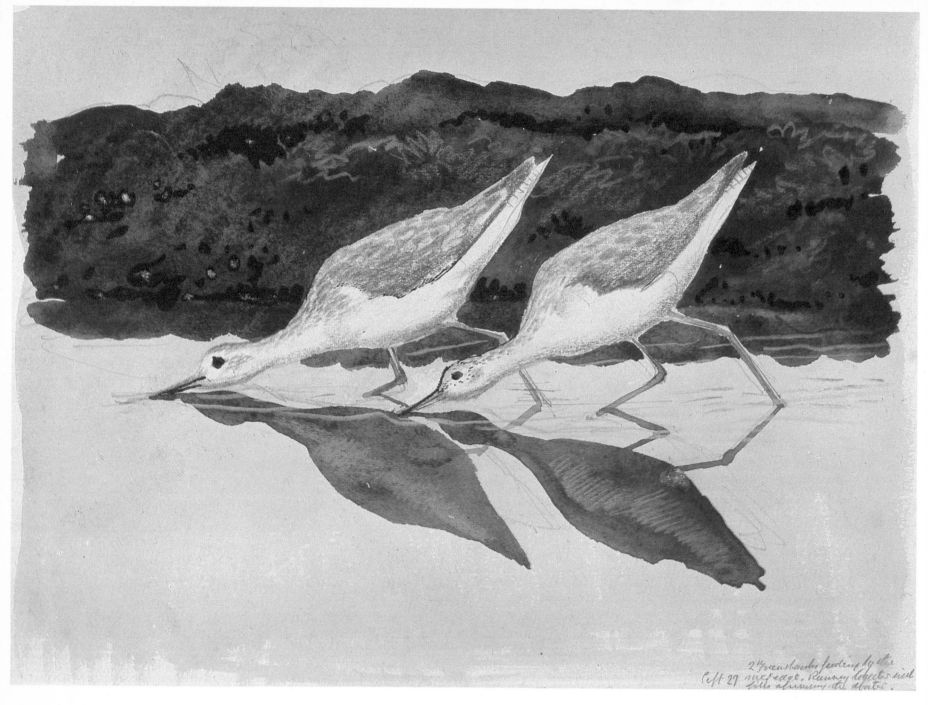

40 Greenshank *Tringa nebularia*, Shorelands, September 29th 1948.

We watch the bend of the river first thing every morning, for some birds are always to be found there, even if they are only the ubiquitous Redshank. They were there in plenty at eight o'clock, running and piping as the rising tide moved them from the little stones in the bed to the sandy edge of the river. But two Greenshanks uttering their own characteristic note, separated from the Redshanks and flew to the opposite side of the river, and there commenced to run along the shore until they were on the stretch opposite the house. There they waded into the water and, laying their bills flat on the surface, they forged ahead, keeping together and almost in step. They did not raise their bills from the water but proceeded parallel to the shore edge, and I think I have never seen anything prettier or more delicate. Soon they reached low seaweedy rocks where they could not continue to run and feed, but among these they pecked and probed, now in full view, now lost in the hollows, but all the time moving towards the road bridge.

Shorelands Summer Diary

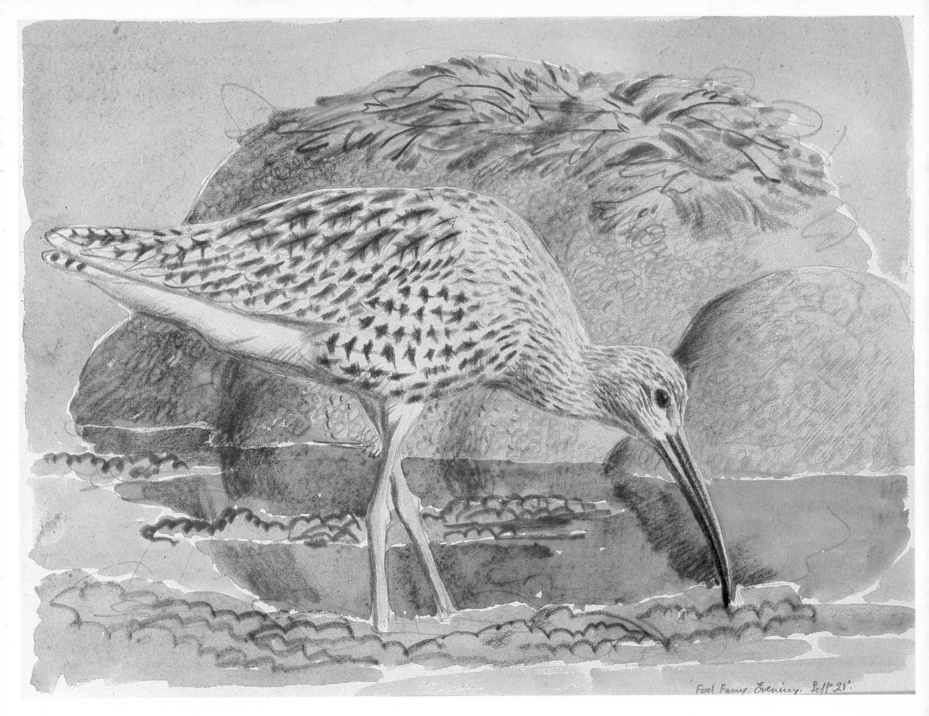

Foel Ferry. Evening. Sept 21.

41 Curlew *Numenius arquata*, Foel Ferry,
September 21st 1948.

A beautiful drawing in colour wash and coloured
crayon: a Curlew feeds in the warm light of
evening, slowly probing the mud with its long
curved bill—a quiet contrast to the busy
Greenshanks opposite.

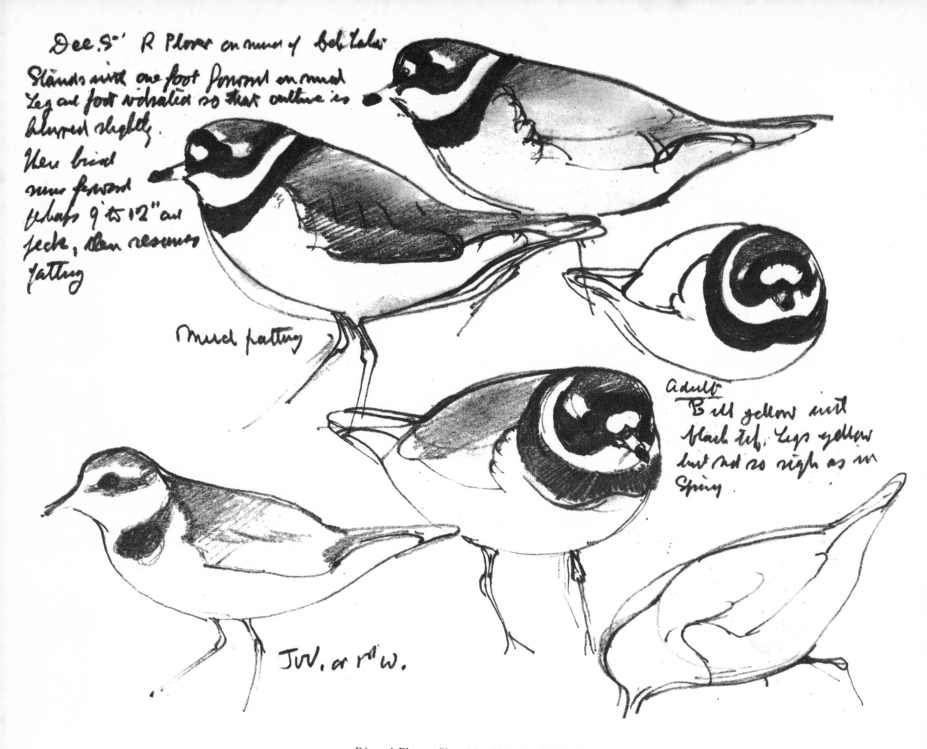

42 Ringed Plover *Charadrius hiaticula*, Cob Lake, December 5th 1956.

Pencil sketches from life in a field sketchbook.

Ringed Plover on mud of Cob Lake. Stands with one foot forward on mud. Leg and foot vibrated so that outline is blurred slightly. Then bird runs forward perhaps 9 to 12 inches and pecks, then resumes patting.

43 Avocet *Recurvirostra avosetta*, Cob Lake, March 29th 1969.

Memory drawings, in line and wash, in a studio sketchbook.

A pair of Avocets feeding, often belly-deep. Not much side-to-side movement of the bill, but a regular prodding of the mud (each ¾ second).

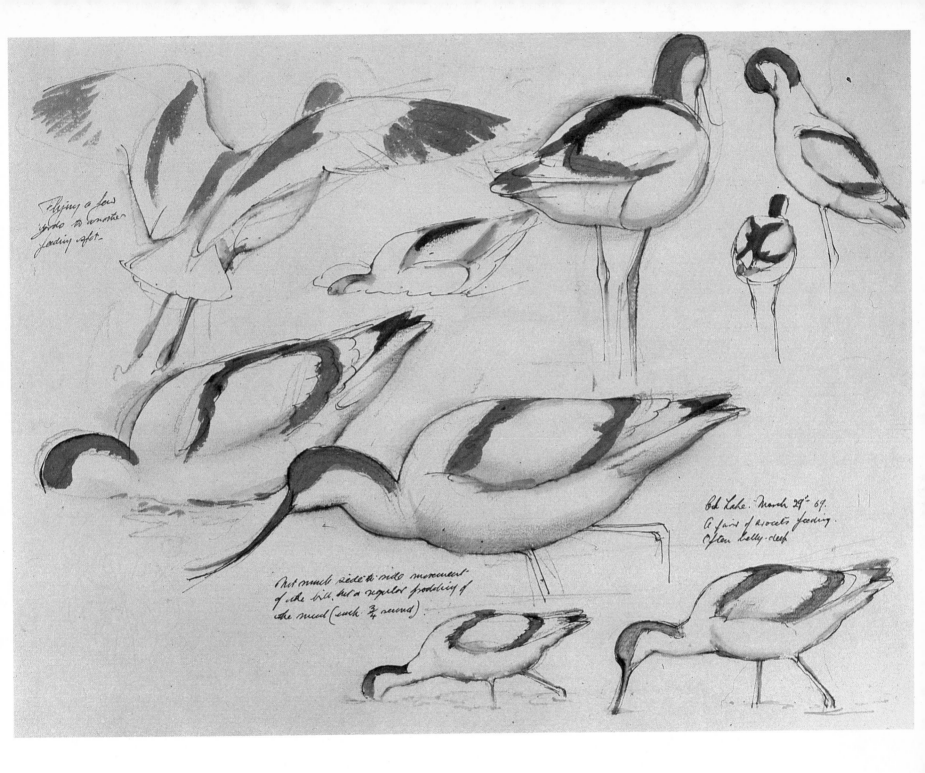

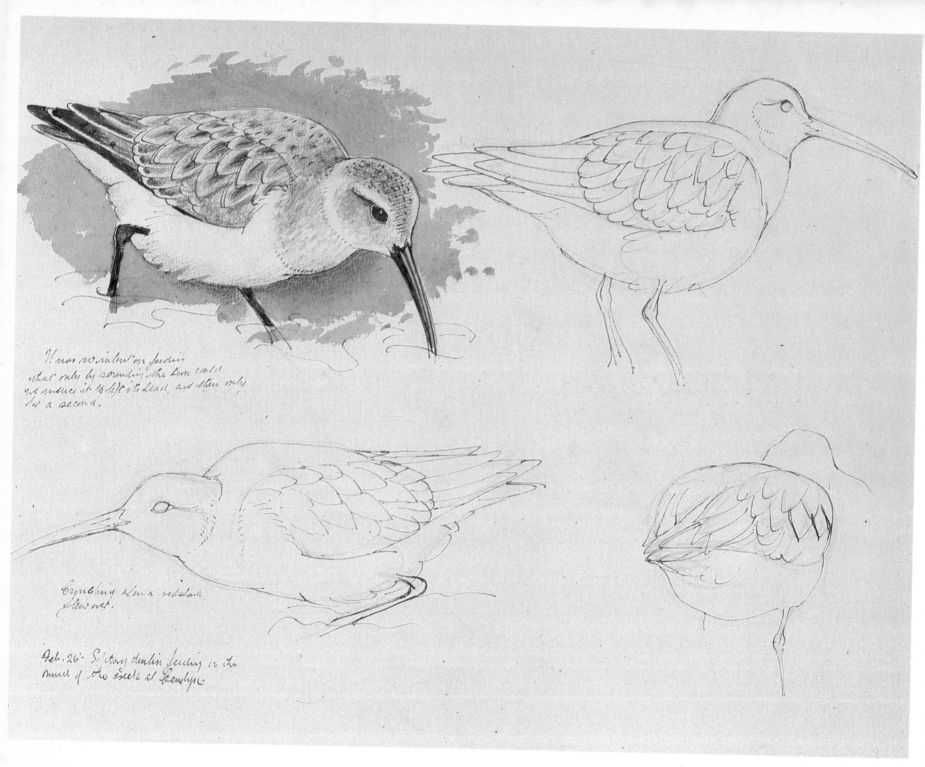

It was so intent on feeding that only by sounding the horn could we induce it to lift its head, and then only for a second.

Crouching when a redshank flew over.

Feb. 26: Solitary dunlin feeding on the mud of the creek at Cemlyn.

44 Dunlin *Calidris alpina*, Cemlyn, February 26th 1956.

Crouching when a Redshank flew over.

It was so intent on feeding that only by sounding the horn could we induce it to lift its head, and then only for a second.

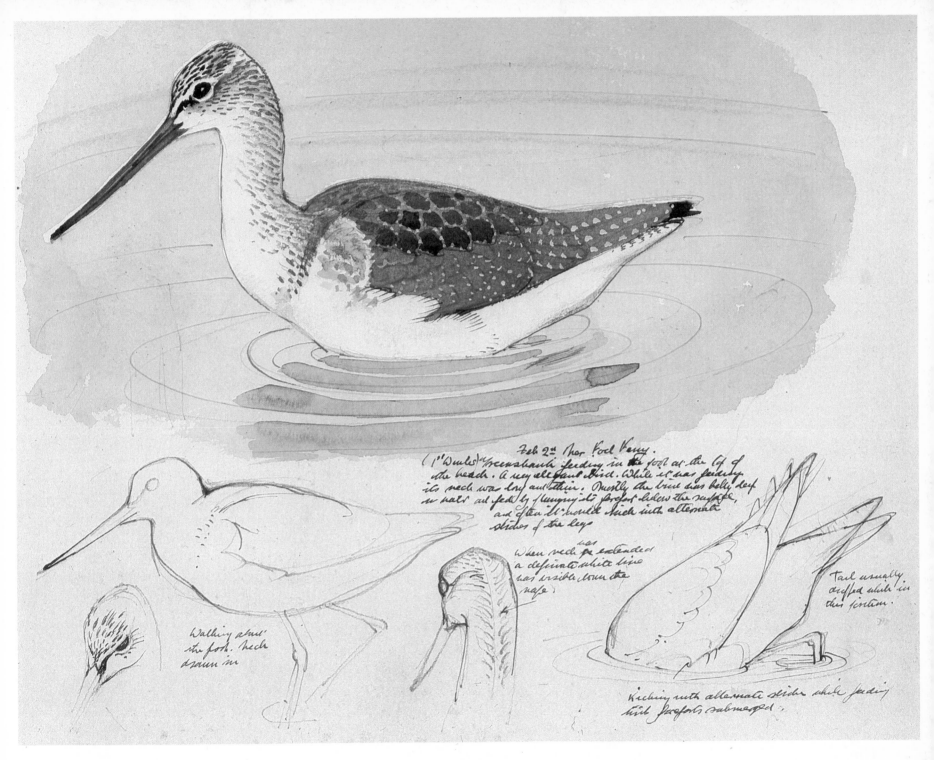

45 Greenshank *Tringa nebularia*, Foel Ferry,
February 2nd 1956.

*(1st winter) Greenshank feeding in the pool at the top of
the beach. A very elegant bird. While it was feeding its*
neck was long and thin. Mostly the bird was belly deep in
water and fed by plunging its forepart below the surface,
and often it would kick with alternate strokes of the legs.
When neck was extended a definite white line was visible
down the nape.

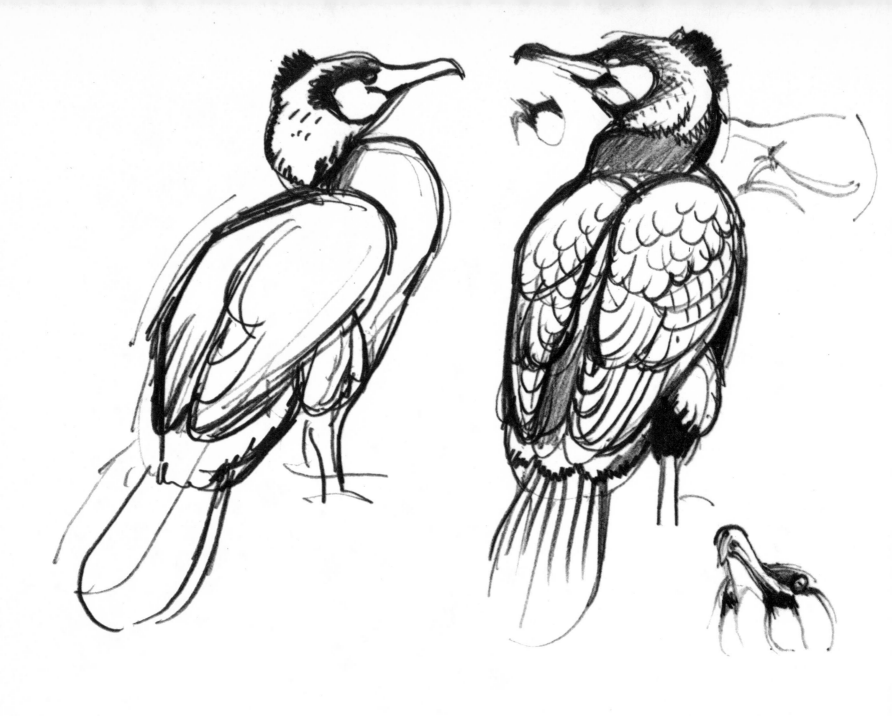

46 Cormorant *Phalacrocorax carbo*, Shorelands, March 24th 1956.

A pencil drawing, made from the studio window, of a pair of Cormorants in full breeding plumage resting on the stony bank in front of Shorelands.

47 Cormorant *Phalacrocorax carbo*, Cob Lake, November 13th 1944.

Cormorant found dead on the shore of Cob Lake. Shot wounds in breast and wings. When found bird had its mouth slightly open. I, thinking I saw the bird's tongue, opened the bill wider and found that the tongue was a fish tail. I pulled and up came a flat fish which measured 8″ from mouth to tail and 3″ across the body not counting the fin width. I brought it home and as the plumage dried it was clear that the bird was in moult for it was entirely dotted with a mixture of old and new feathers. Tail, wings, coverts, scapulars etc, all were in this state of transition.

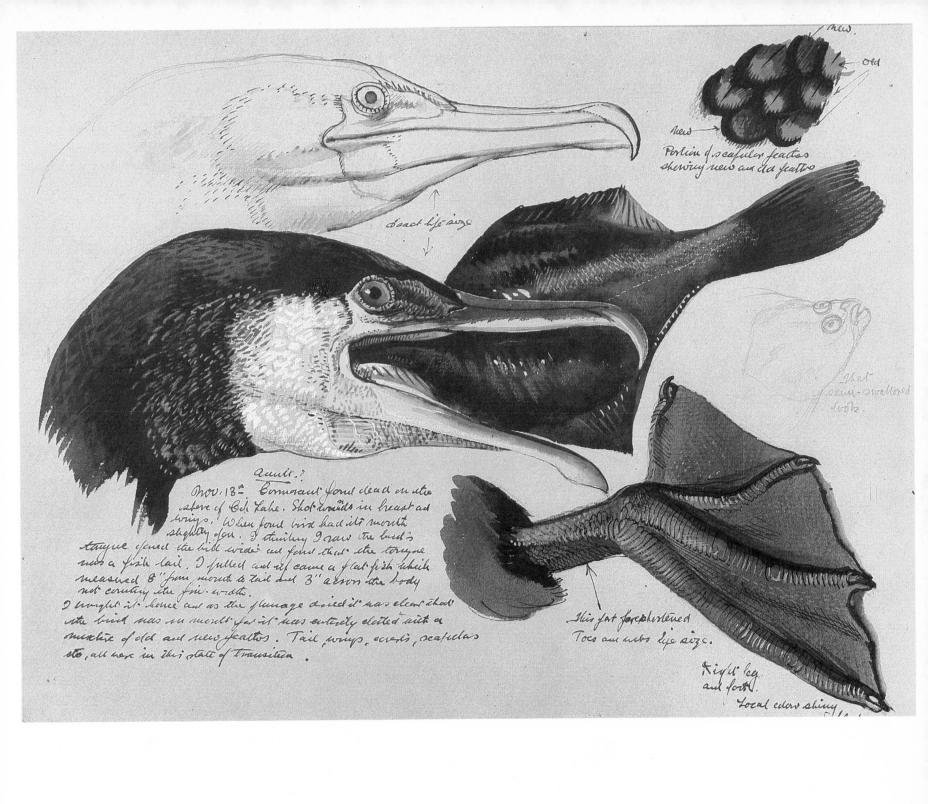

New.

Old

New

Portion of scapular feathers
shewing new and old feathers

exact life size

that
semi-swallowed
look.

Adult?

Nov. 13th Cormorant found dead on the
shore of Och Lake. Shot wounds in breast and
wings. When found bird had its mouth
slightly open. I thinking I saw the bird's
tongue opened the bill wider and found that the tongue
was a fish tail. I pulled and up came a flat fish which
measured 8" from mouth to tail and 3" across the body
not counting the fin-width.
I brought it home and as the plumage dried it was clear that
the bird was in moult for it was entirely clothed with a
mixture of old and new feathers. Tail, wings, coverts, scapulars
etc, all were in this state of transition.

This foot foreshortened
Toes are under life size.

Right leg
and foot.
Local colour shiny

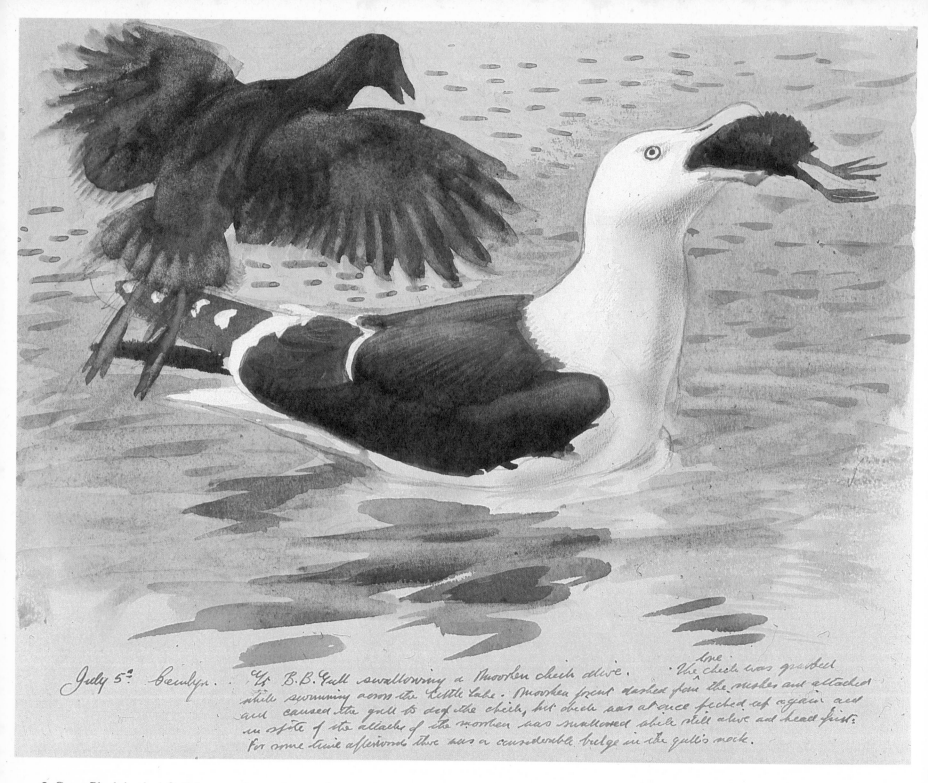

July 5th Cemlyn. G.B.B. Gull swallowing a Moorhen chick alive. The chick was grabbed while swimming across the Little Lake. Moorhen parent dashed from the rushes and attacked and caused the gull to drop the chick, but chick was at once picked up again and in spite of the attacks of the moorhen was swallowed while still alive and head first. For some time afterwards there was a considerable bulge in the gull's neck.

48 Great Black-backed Gull *Larus marinus* and Moorhen *Gallinula chloropus*, Cemlyn, July 5th 1958.

Two dramatic encounters involving the Great Black-backed Gull—a notorious pirate and scavenger. I suspect that these incidents were more interesting to Tunnicliffe as aspects of bird behaviour than as potential subjects for paintings.

Great Black-backed Gull swallowing a Moorhen chick alive. The lone chick was grabbed while swimming across the Little Lake. Moorhen parent dashed from the rushes and attacked and caused the gull to drop the chick, but chick was at once picked up again and in spite of the attacks of the Moorhen was swallowed while still alive and head first. For some time afterwards there was a considerable bulge in the gull's neck.

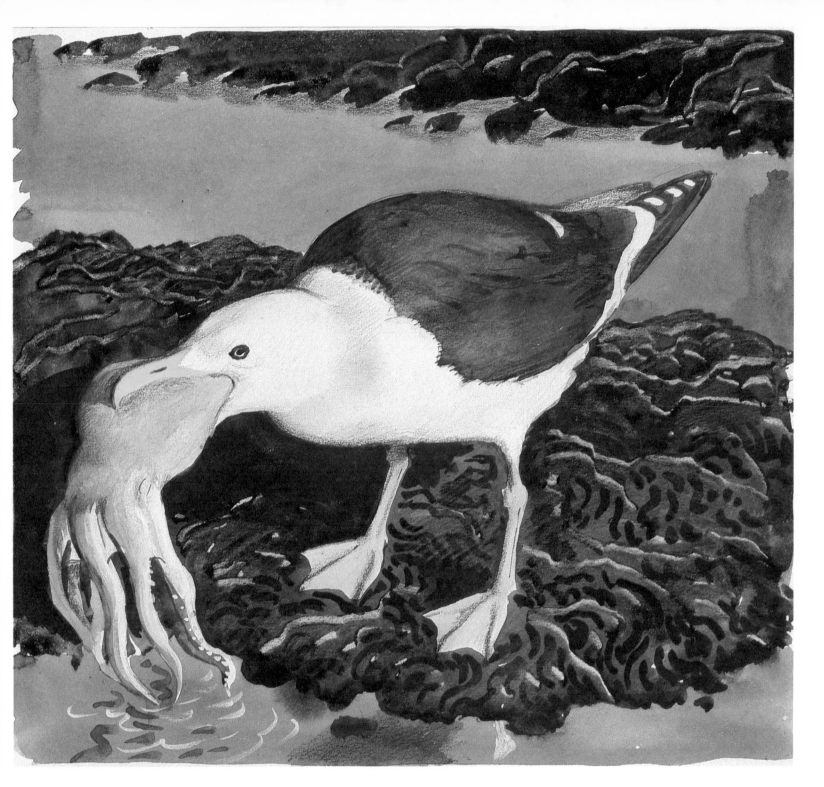

49 Great Black-backed Gull *Larus marinus*, Foel Ferry, January 5th 1958.

A Great Black-back was seen to drag something onto the seaweed and to peck and worry it. This was found to be a dead octopus or a squid which the gull tried to swallow whole, though while we watched it did not succeed in doing so. The surprising thing was that when a Heron flew and alighted near, the Black-back immediately dropped the octopus and flew some yards away. The Heron was not interested in the dead octopus and the gull returned to stab and worry. A second time the Heron moved towards the gull and again it at once gave way and did not challenge the Heron in any way. Obviously the Heron is the master bird in these circumstances.

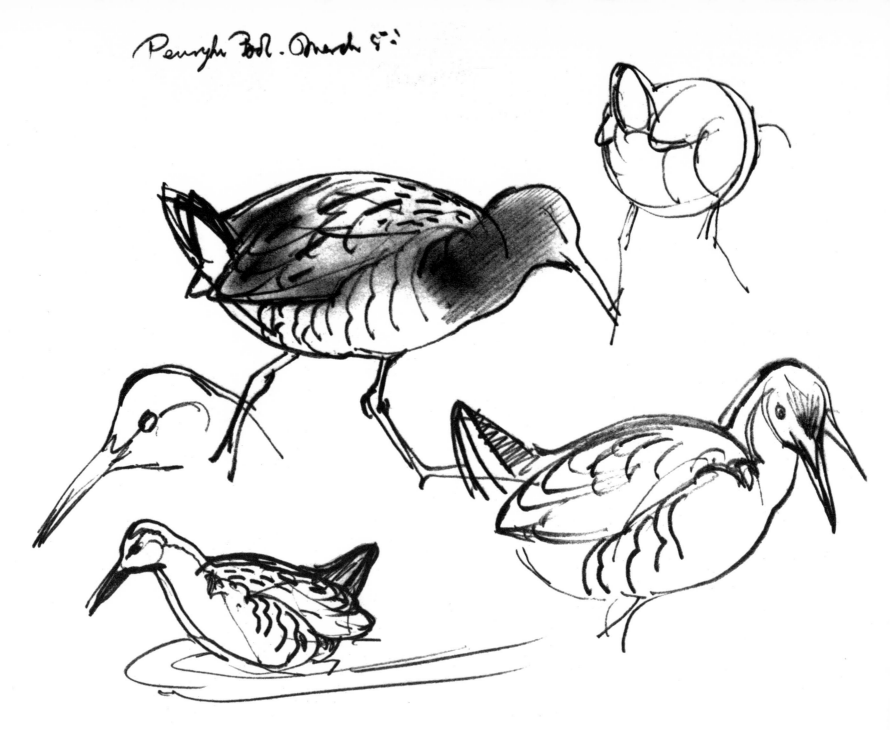

Penryhn Pool. March 5ᵗʰ

50 and **51** Water Rail *Rallus aquaticus*, Penryhn Pool, March 5th 1956.

Pencil field sketches of a Water Rail, feeding by the rushy shore of a swampy pool near Penryhn Castle. These sketches were used later the same day to make the studio sketch in colour opposite. Some tentative pencil sketches have been firmed-up with a clear pen line.

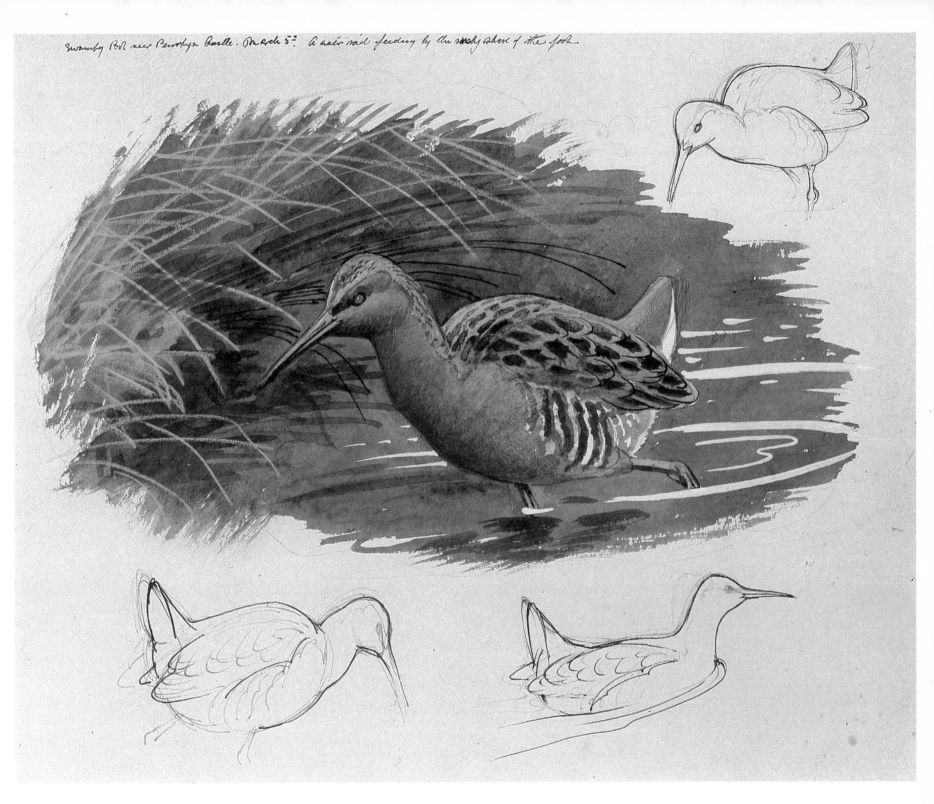

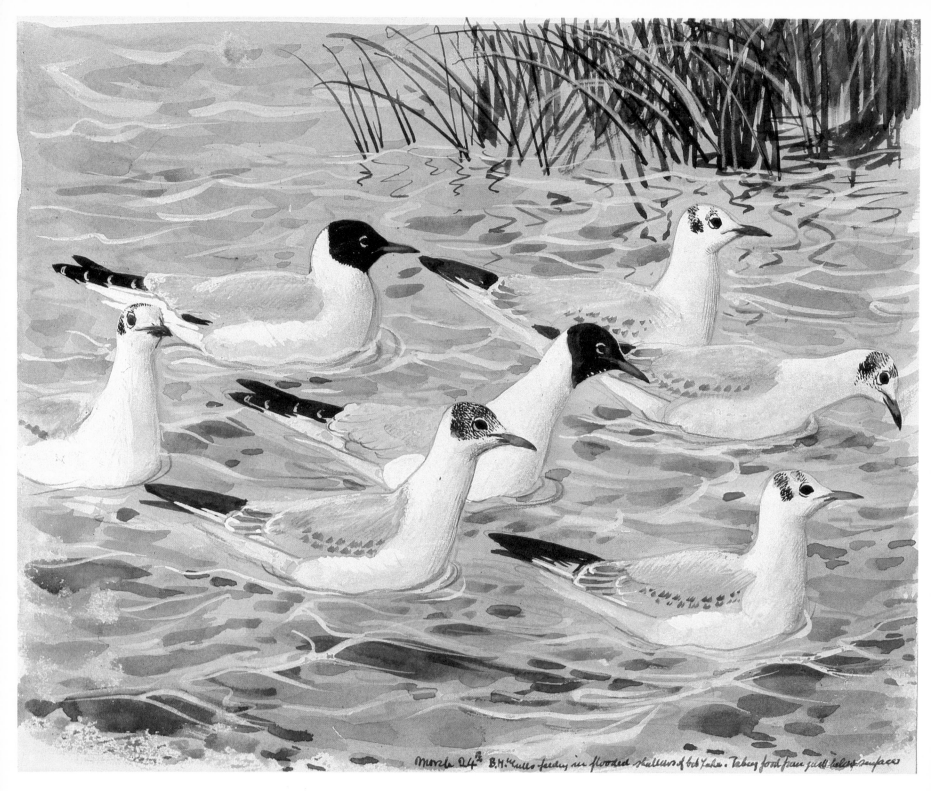

March 24th B.H. Gulls feeding in flooded shallows of Cob Lake. Taking food from just below surface

52 Black-headed Gull *Larus ridibundus*, Cob Lake, March 24th 1951.

Black-headed Gulls feeding in flooded shallows of Cob Lake. Taking food from just below surface.

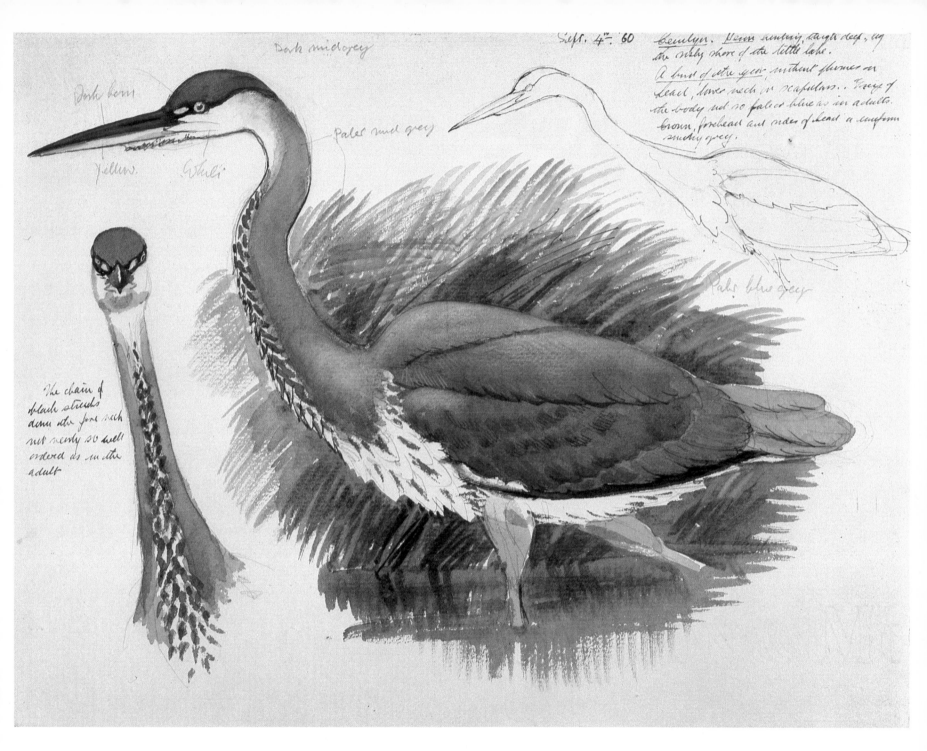

Dark midgrey

Dark horn

Yellow. White.

Paler mid grey

Sept. 4ᵗʰ '60

Cemlyn. Heron hunting thigh deep, up the rushy shore of the little lake.
A bird of the year, without plumes on head, lower neck or scapulars. Grey of the body not so pale or blue as in adults. Crown, forehead and sides of head a uniform smoky grey.

Pale blue grey

The chain of black streaks down the fore neck not nearly so well ordered as in the adult

53 Heron *Ardea cinerea*, Cemlyn Lake, September 4th 1960.

Heron hunting thigh deep, by the rushy shore of the Little Lake. A bird of the year, without plumes on head, lower neck or scapulars. Grey of the body not so pale or blue as in adults. Crown, forehead and sides of head a uniform smoky grey. The chain of black streaks down the fore neck not nearly so well ordered in the adult.

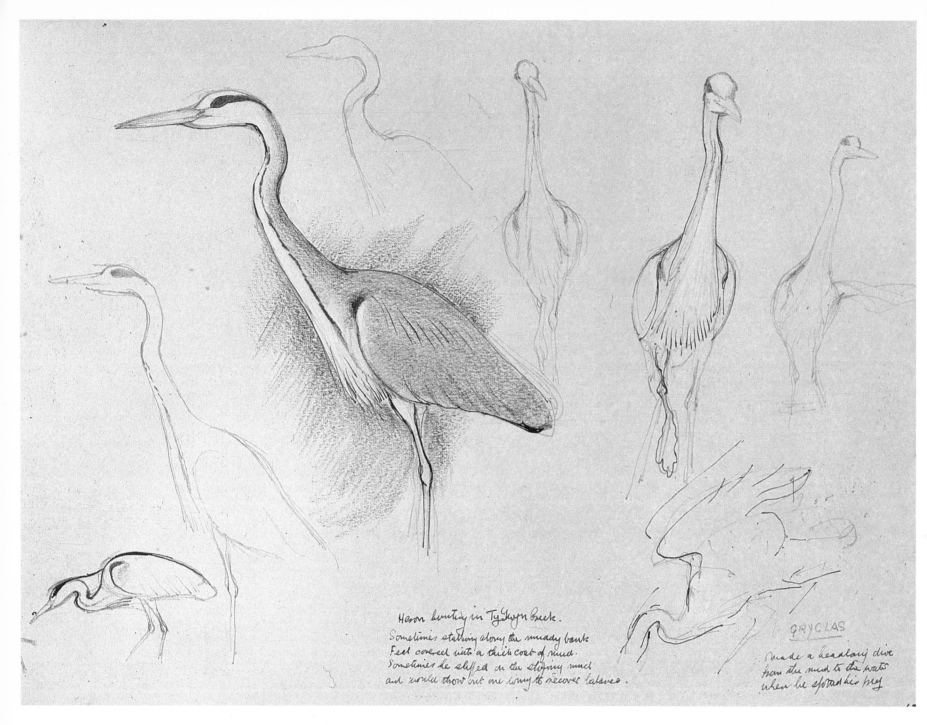

Heron hunting in Ty Gwyn Creek.

Sometimes stalking along the muddy bank.
Feet covered with a thick coat of mud.
Sometimes he slipped on the sloping mud
and would throw out one wing to recover balance.

GRYGLAS

Made a headlong dive
from the mud to the water
when he spotted his prey

54 Heron *Ardea cinerea*, Ty Gwyn Creek, May
1945.

*Sometimes stalking along the muddy bank. Feet covered
with a thick coat of mud. Sometimes he slipped on the
sloping mud and would throw out one wing to recover
balance. Made a headlong dive from the mud to the water
when he spotted his prey.*

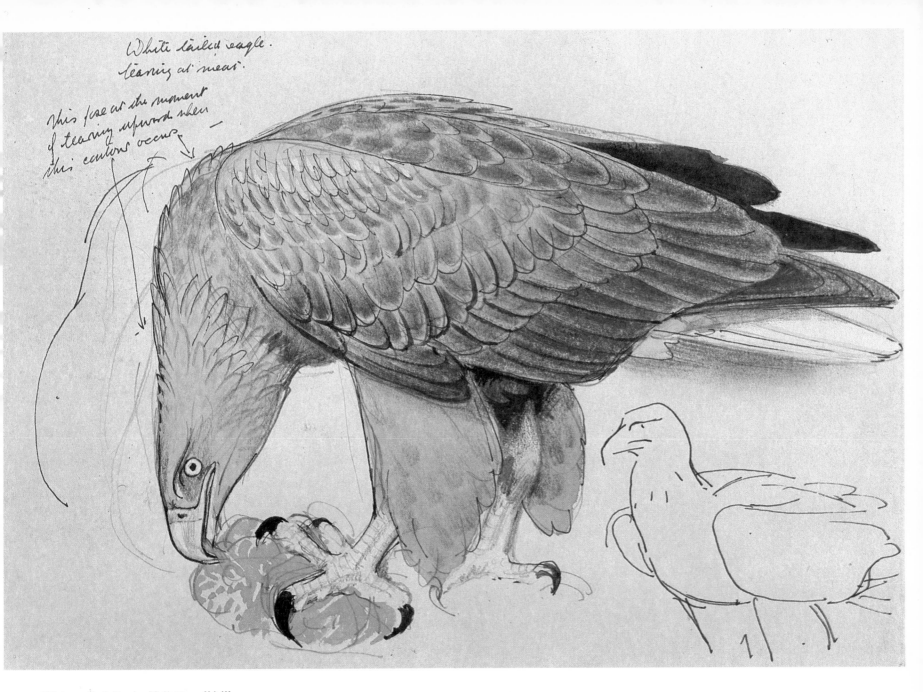

55 White-tailed Eagle *Haliaëtus albicilla*.

This is an undated zoo study of a White-tailed
Eagle feeding on raw meat.

*This pose at the moment of tearing upward when this
contour occurs.*

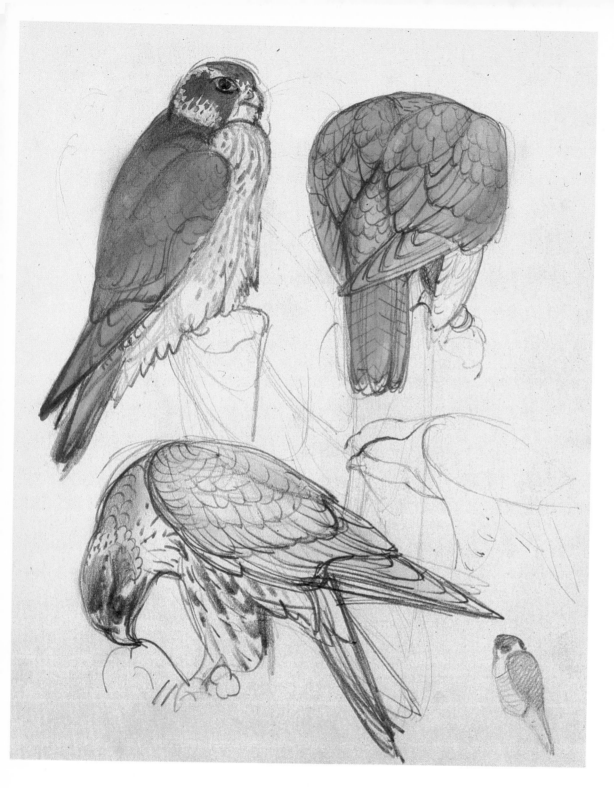

56 and **57** Gyrfalcon *Falco rusticolus*, belonging to Ronald Stevens Esq, mid August 1951.

Female Gyr feeding on the glove. When being transferred from block to indoor perches they were fed on the glove. Mr S. told me that their grip was not strong and that at times he had difficulty in balancing the heavy bird on his glove. The Gyrs were put under a lean-to, open-sided shed at night. Peregrines were taken indoors.

Two of a series of sketches, later used for the watercolour in the Royal Academy, 1952, entitled *The one from Norway*, and for another painting which decorates the dust jacket of *The Taming of Genghis*, 1966, an account by Ronald Stevens of his relationship with a Gyrfalcon.

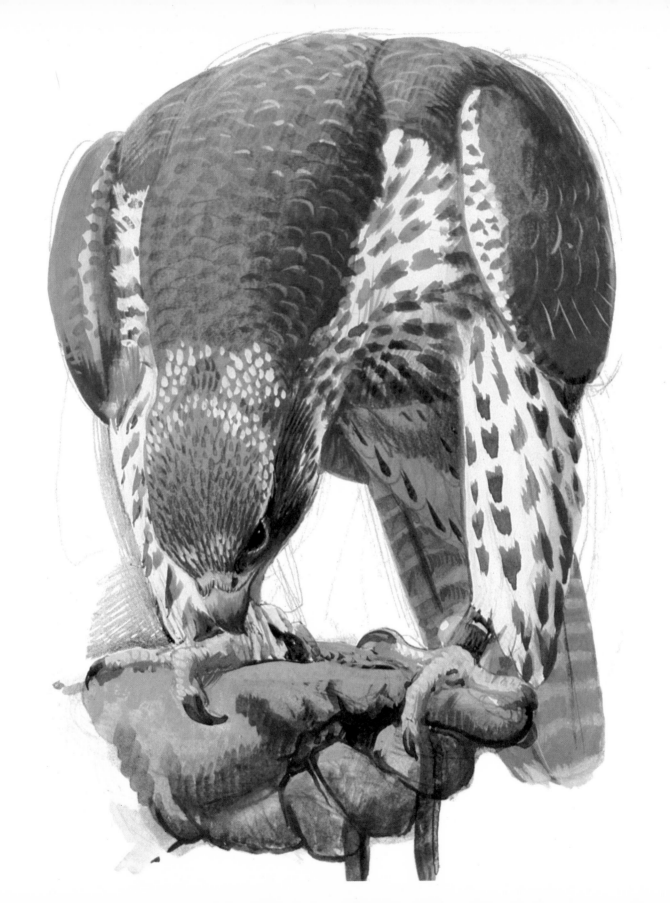

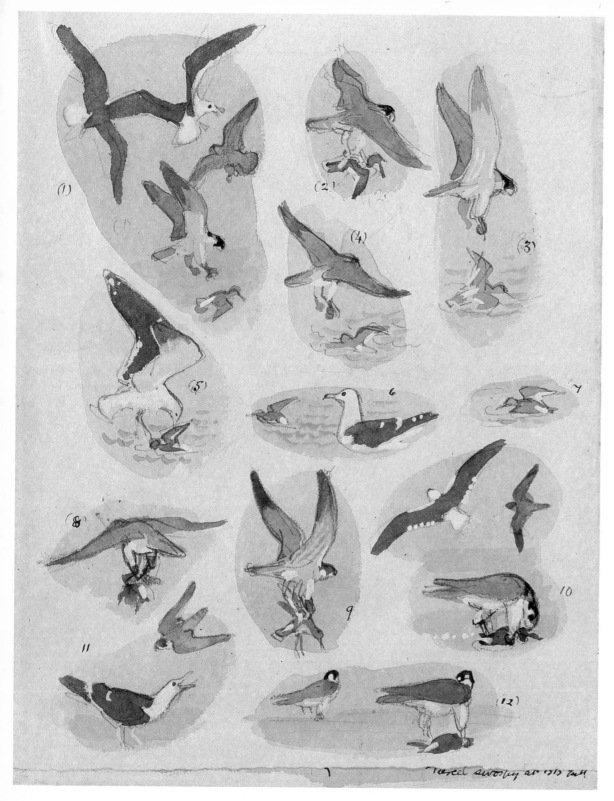

58 and **59** Peregrine *Falco peregrinus*, with injured Redshank *Tringa totanus*, Shorelands, December 18th 1954.

First saw a flurry of wings on the sand between the Cob and the river. (1) Black-backed Gulls and a pair of Peregrines disputing possession of a Redshank staggering on the sand with a broken wing and leg. (2) The larger falcon clutched the Redshank, carried it a few feet, then let it drop. Clutched it again, carried it, and dropped it into the shallows of the river. (3) Meanwhile the smaller P. swooped and stooped at the BB Gulls. The Redshank struggled in the shallows and the larger falcon made several attempts to fasten (4) on to it but appeared afraid of the water and lifted up without binding on to the Redshank. Then both Peregrines sat on the sands. (5) A BB Gull then attacked the floundering Redshank dropping on it several times without actually attempting to kill it (which it could easily have done). The Redshank floundered away from the gull which sat in the water (6) and watched. Redshank reached the shallows and there seemed to collapse (7). The larger Peregrine now flew up, grabbed the Redshank and took it onto the sands away from the river edge (8). At one stage of the transport the Peregrine appeared to be holding it by the wings with the body hanging limp below (9). On the sand again the large Peregrine straddled the R. and began to pluck and jab (10). Little stream of feathers trailed away from the R. The smaller P. did not attempt to approach the feeding P. but occupied itself in chasing all other gulls and crows away from the feeding bird. Having accomplished this after some fine flying at the gulls in the air and some stooping at them as they stood on the sands (11) the smaller P. rested on the sand not far from its feeding mate (12). This larger bird took its fill then moved off the prey and the smaller P. took its place and commenced to feed. No other birds now disputed the Peregrine's right to the R. and the larger P. just rested on the sands while the smaller fed. He took his fill and moved off and for a time both Peregrines stood on the sands. Then the larger P. came to the prey again and ate a little more. The smaller P. suddenly appeared to be trying to vomit and was no doubt ejecting a pellet. His head moved up and down with bill pointing downward. I did not see him eject anything. Later the Peregrine flew off and the Crows took possession of the remains of the Redshank.

Dull cloudy day. Wind from the south. Several shooters about. Redshank probably a shot bird.

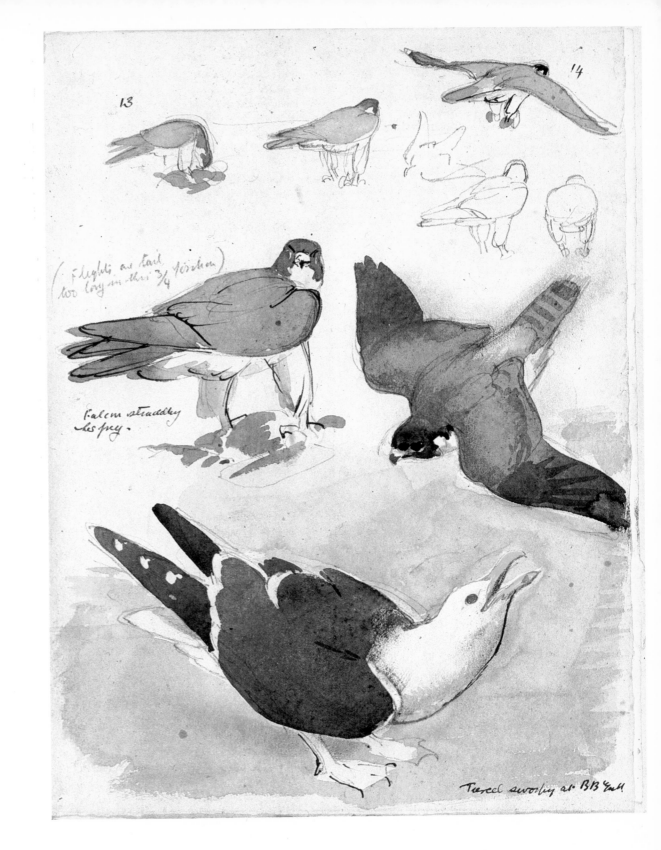

13

14

(flights are tail
too long in this 3/4 position)

Falcon straddling
his prey.

Tiercel swooping at B B Gull

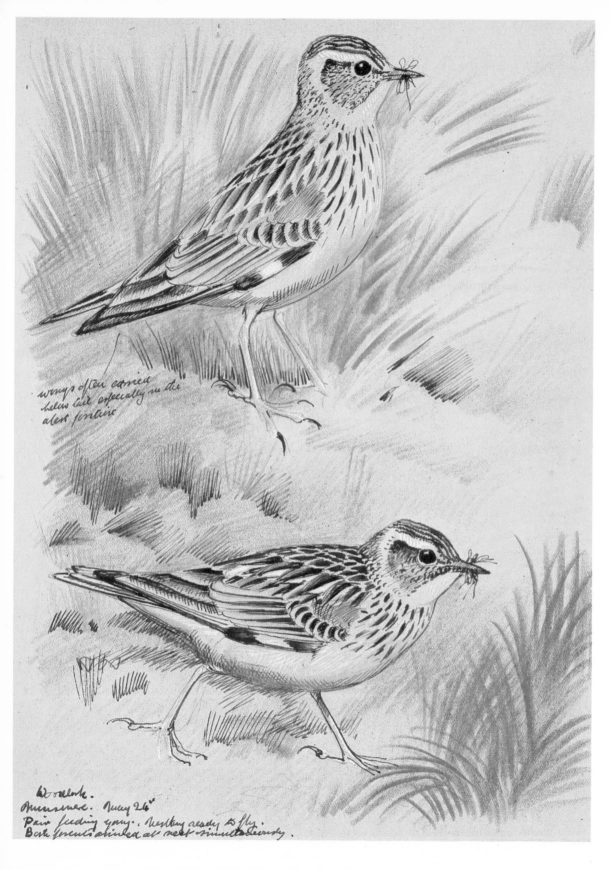

60 Woodlark *Lullula arborea*, Minsmere, May 24th 1950.

Pair feeding young. Nestling ready to fly. Both parents arrived at nest simultaneously.

Tunnicliffe has drawn the pair of Woodlarks, watched from a hide on the R.S.P.B. reserve, in two typical postures, adding the following note to the upper bird.

Wings often carried below tail especially in the alert posture.

61 Black-necked Grebe *Podiceps nigricollis*, Foel
Ferry, February 13th 1955.

*Swallowing a fish, a long ribbon-like fish, about six
inches long. Swallowed with some effort. When first seen
flank feathers very fluffed up at the rear. The red eye seen
in certain lights. On Feb. 14th there was a B.N. Grebe
at the same place, and at the same state of the tide.*

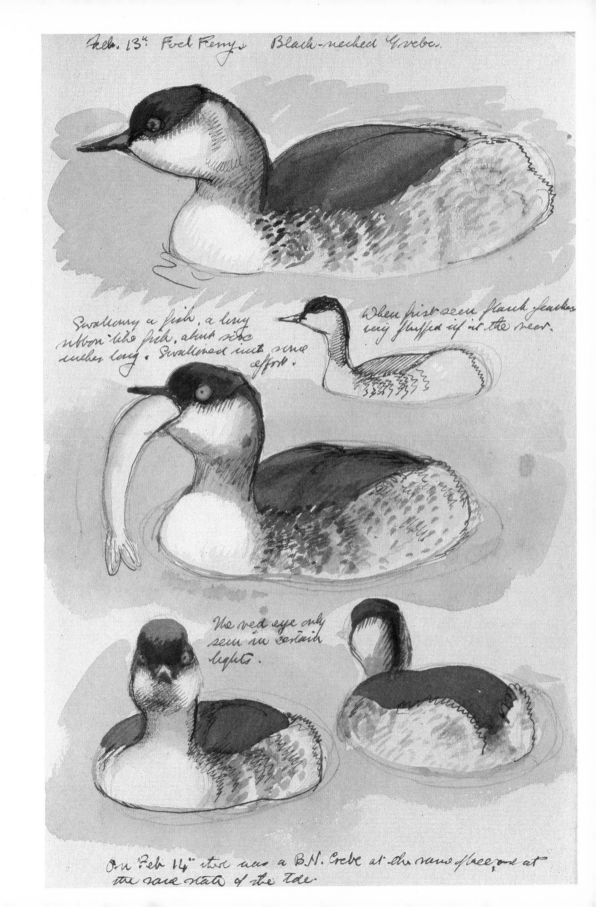

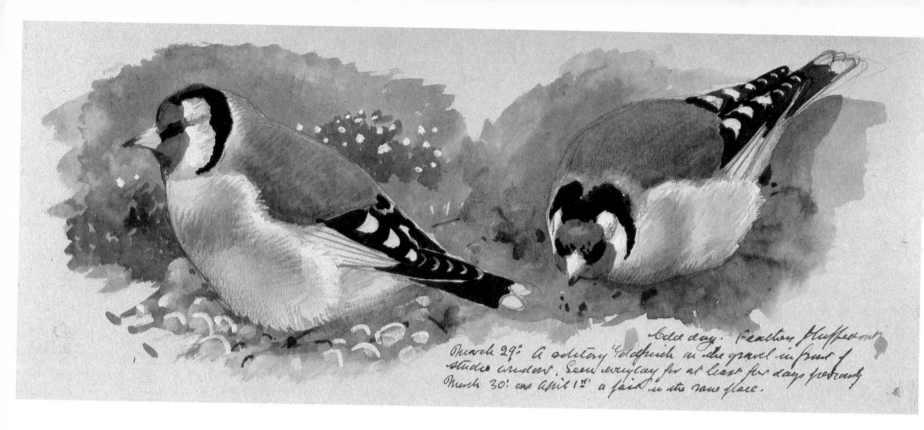

March 29: A solitary Goldfinch on the gravel in front of studio window. Seen every day for at least five days previously. March 30: and April 1st a pair in the same place.

Cold day. Feathers fluffed out.

62 Goldfinch *Carduelis carduelis*, Shorelands, March 29th 1956.

A solitary Goldfinch on the gravel in front of studio window. Cold day. Feathers fluffed out. Seen every day for at least four days previously, March 30th and April 1st a pair in the same place.

Flying

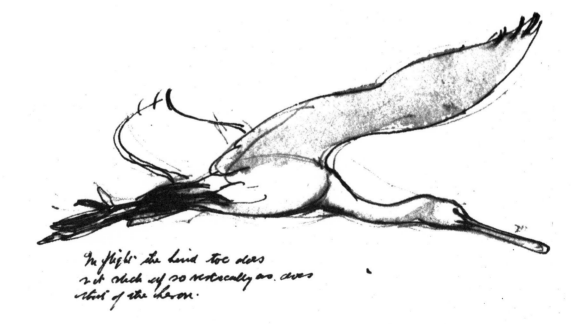

In flight the hind toe does
not stick up so vertically as does
that of the heron.

In *Bird Portraiture* Tunnicliffe wrote "I am sure that, sooner or later, you will become engrossed in the study of the flying bird, and be filled with wonder at the beauty of its shape as it soars, glides, swoops, or speeds on its way." This certainly happened to Tunnicliffe. His sketchbooks are full of birds in flight—some are very simple, quick sketches to record a momentary impression while others are finished drawings, both in detail and colour. All reflect that fascination which the flying bird has exerted on man, ever since he was first able to comprehend the wonder of bird flight.

Some of the drawings that follow could have been placed in the section on feeding as they show birds engaged in hunting, but it is the flying element in them that is highlighted—the focal point of Tunnicliffe's attention when making the drawings. Most of these pages have numerous sketches—flying birds are constantly changing aspect and the artist can never catch up, no matter how many different positions he tries to capture. Some of the sketches are tentative and we can sense the artist searching for the right line to express the movement. Some are bold and almost diagrammatic, like those of a Short-eared Owl (**70**) for example, showing Tunnicliffe's concern with proportion and shape as he tried to put down the essential character of the bird and its particular mode of flight without bothering over detail. The page of Ravens, sketched in aerial play above their roost (**68**), were first drawn with pencil, the line seeking and developing the shapes he had memorised. They were then filled in with brush and ink, pinning down the positions in a series of bold silhouettes.

Tunnicliffe constantly annotated his sketches with notes that would be invaluable to him when read later, perhaps much later, in the studio. There are also many notes, such as those added to the drawing of alighting Bewick's Swans (**66**), which might not be immediately relevant to picture making but which reveal his keen powers of observation and interest in the minutiae of bird life and behaviour.

There are three examples of hunting methods which show how different birds of prey have sighted, stooped and captured their quarry. The first, of a Kestrel (**64**), drawn in 1938, was done on the spot from direct observation in the field. (See also **65** and **73**.) Tunnicliffe had an outstandingly quick eye for seeing a sequence of movements, and a very quick pencil with which to record them. In this he matched the Swedish painter Bruno Liljefors, whom Tunnicliffe greatly admired as one of the greatest animal artists of all time. Liljefors did many remarkable pictures of birds in flight, especially birds of prey and seabirds, at a time when there were no photographs to aid him. He relied on a phenomenal eye for isolating dramatic moments of high-speed action. One cannot help thinking Liljefors would have recognised Tunnicliffe as a kindred spirit.

Previous page: Spoonbill *Platalea leucorodia*

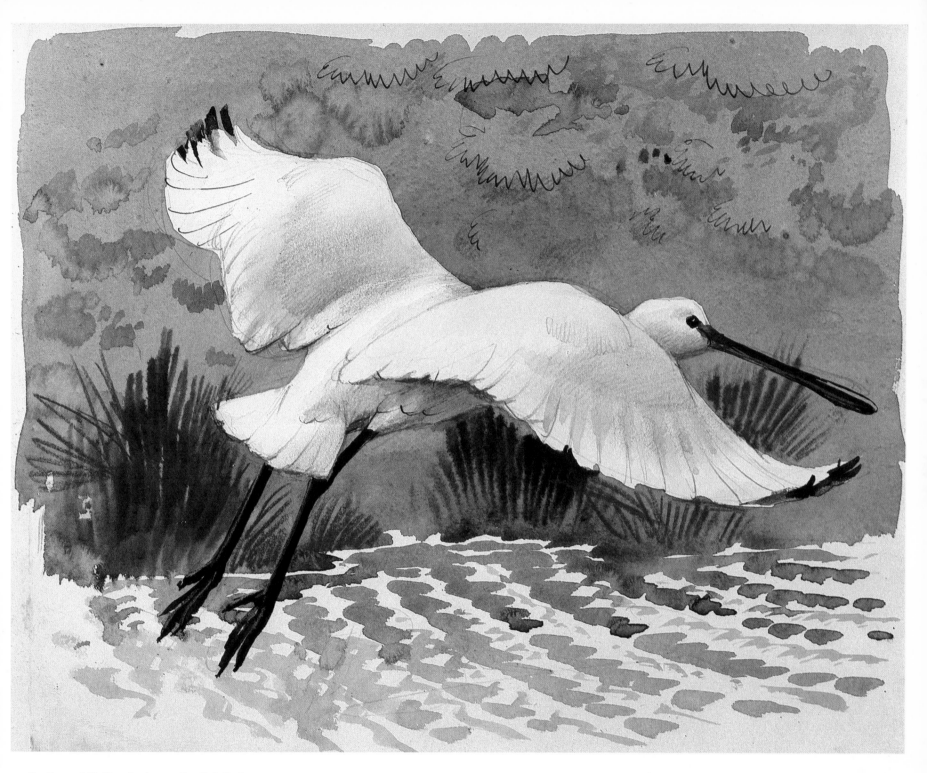

63 Spoonbill *Platalea leucorodia*, Cob Lake,
December 10th 1955.

A young bird taking off and flying along the edge
of the lake.

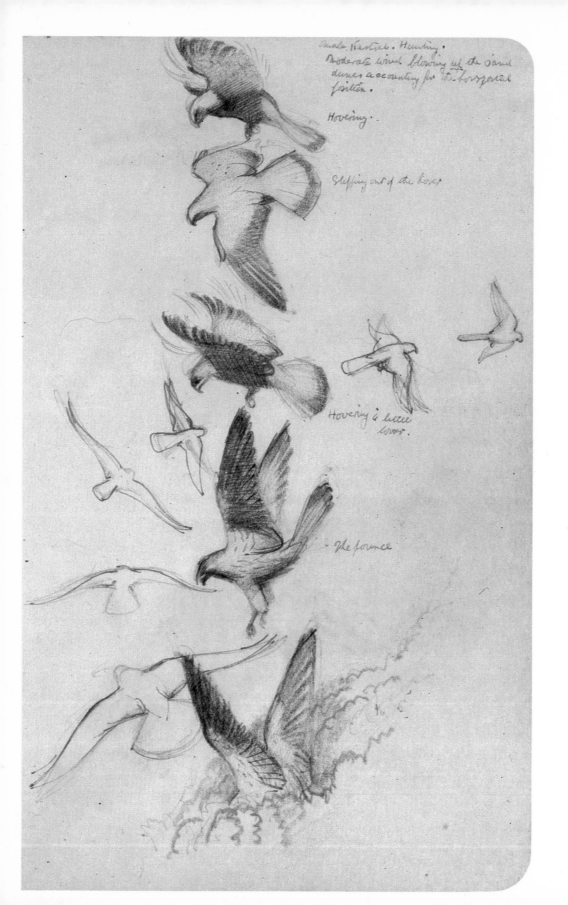

64 Kestrel *Falco tinnunculus*, June 16th 1938.

Male Kestrel. Hunting. Moderate wind blowing up the sand dunes accounting for the horizontal position.

Tunnicliffe made use of this series of sketches of a hunting Kestrel for one of the illustrations in his *Bird Portraiture*, 1945.

For further understanding of their action it is a good plan, sometimes, to draw, in sequence, a bird's movements as they actually occur: for instance, in watching a Kestrel hunting you would naturally begin with a sketch of the hovering position; then a quick note of its appearance as it slips out of the hover to descend a little lower; then another hovering note, which may not be quite the same as the first because the bird may be hovering in a different current of air; then the quick descent on to its prey; and, last of all, its action as it beats up from its find. You may see it rise with a mouse dangling from one foot, or even a young rabbit. When you have recorded such a sequence of movements you will feel that you know a little more about the appearance of the bird.

Bird Portraiture.

65 Barn Owl *Tyto alba*, Brereton, January 7th (? year).

Barn Owl hunting and making its kill in the field below the drive at Brereton Church Gate. Hunting in a good light at 2 pm to 2.30 (no sunlight).

1. Flying through the trees.

2. Hunting the field.

3. Hunting intently a few feet above the grass.

4. Hunting.

5. Sudden drop on to its prey.

6. Covering its prey, wings spread.

7. Quick downward jabs at its prey, presumably killing with its beak.

8. Up on its feet, prey, probably mouse or vole, dangling from beak.

9. Swallowing prey with quick spasmodic jerks of head.

10. After prey had disappeared whole, stood and rested for several minutes. (Tail seemed to be carried clear of the ground when standing.)

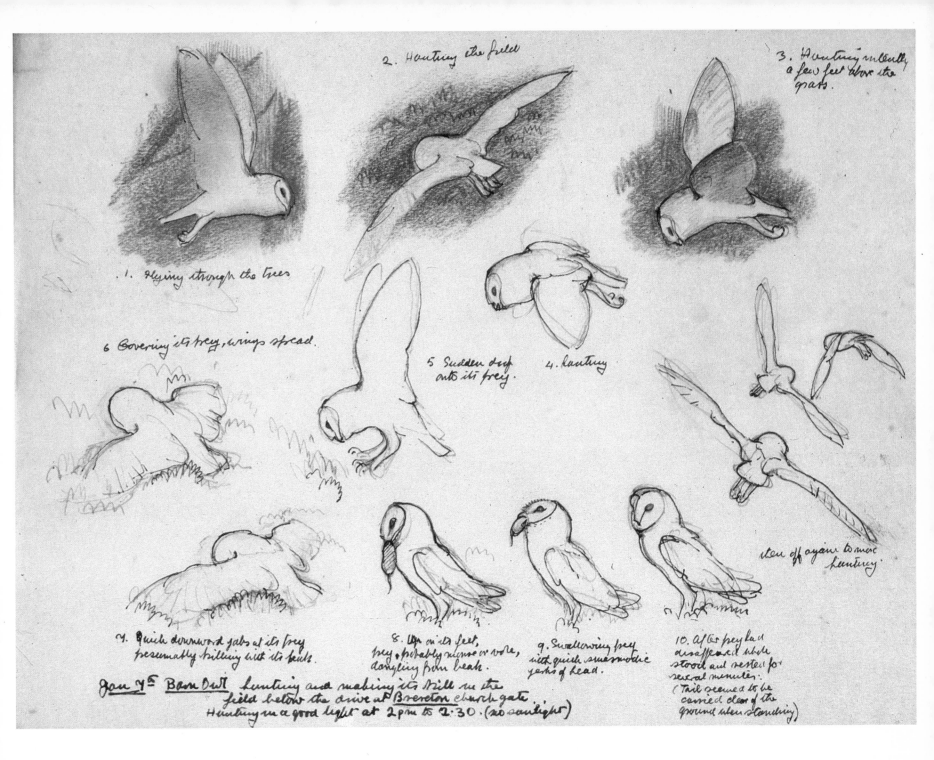

2. Hunting the field

3. Hunting intently a few feet above the grass.

1. Flying through the trees

6 Covering its prey, wings spread.

5 Sudden drop onto its prey.

4. hunting

then off again to more hunting

7. Quick downward jabs at its prey presumably killing with its beak.

8. Up on its feet, prey, probably mouse or vole, dangling from beak.

9. Swallowing prey with quick spasmodic jerks of head.

10. After prey had disappeared whole stood and rested for several minutes. (Tail seemed to be carried clear of the ground when standing.)

Jan 9th Barn Owl hunting and making its kill in the field below the drive at Brereton church gate. Hunting in a good light at 2pm to 2.30. (no sunlight)

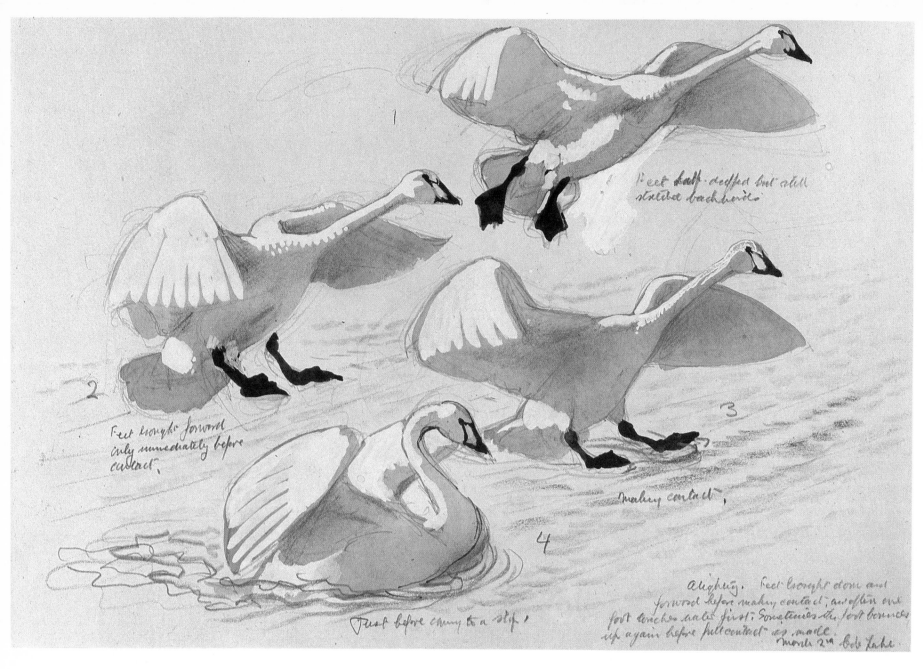

1

Feet half-dropped but still stretched backwards.

2

Feet brought forward only immediately before contact.

3

making contact.

4

Just before coming to a stop.

alighting. Feet brought down and forward before making contact, and often one foot touches water first. Sometimes the foot bounces up again before full contact is made.

March 2nd. Cob Lake.

66 Bewick's Swan _Cygnus bewickii_, alighting, Cob Lake, March 2nd 1949.

Feet brought down and forward before making contact, and often one foot touches water first. Sometimes the foot bounces up again before full contact is made.

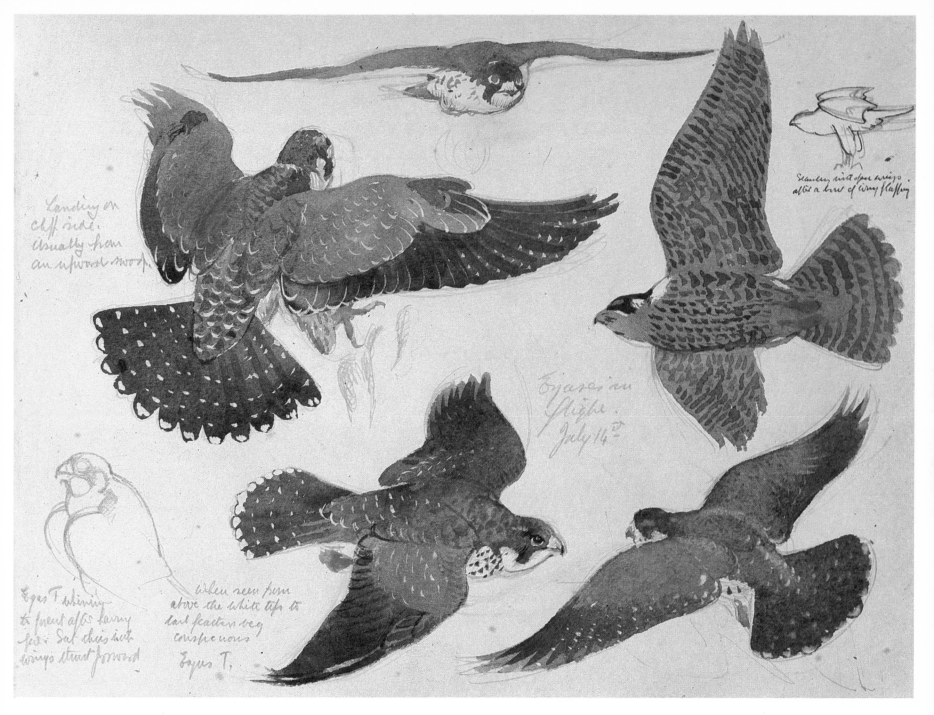

Landing on
cliff side.
Usually from
an upward swoop.

Standing with open wings
after a bout of wing flapping

Eyass in
flight.
July 14th

When seen from
above the white tips to
tail feathers very
conspicuous
Eyas T.

Eyes T whining
to front after being
fed. Sat thus with
wings stemt forward

67 Peregrine *Falco peregrinus*, South Stack, July
14th 1948.

*For several minutes no Peregrines were to be seen, and, as
expected, the nest was empty, but soon a dark sharp-
winged shape was glimpsed as it showed against the blue
water and we saw that it was one of the eyesses. The pale
tips of its tail feathers were very conspicuous as it opened
them to swoop up the cliff. The eyess attempted to alight
on a ledge but, misjudging its landing, heeled over and
dropped down and out from the cliff to make another
swoop up, this time to alight on a little ledge where a
patch of heather was in bloom. What perfection of
plumage was his! (for it was the male eyess). From
cream-tipped tail to dark crown not a feather was out of
place. His finely modelled back shone in the sun, and his
dark watchful eyes gleamed as he turned his head to
regard us.*

Shorelands Summer Diary.

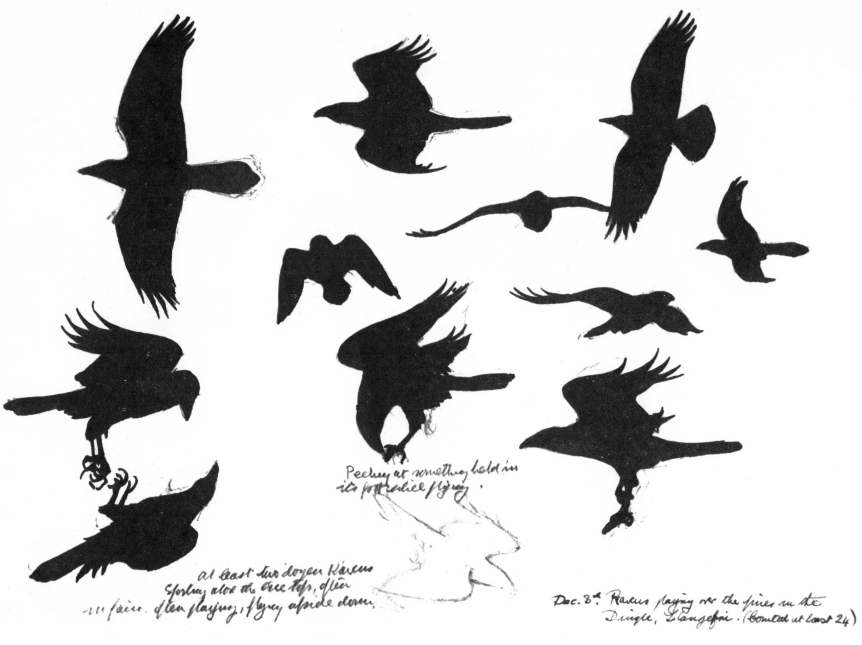

At least two dozen Ravens
sporting above the tree tops, often
in pairs, often playing, flying upside down.

Peeking at something held in
its foot while flying.

Dec. 8th Ravens playing over the pines in the
Dingle, Llangefni. (Counted at least 24)

68 Raven *Corvus corax*, the Dingle, Llangefni,
December 8th 1949.

At least two dozen Ravens sporting above the tree tops,
often in pairs, often playing, flying upside down.

69 Raven *Corvus corax*, South Stack, March 29th
and 30th 1951.

A pair of Ravens with a nest near the lighthouse steps.
The nest, placed in a large triangular niche in a sheer
face of rock consisted mainly of heather with finer material
for a lining. Could not see into the cup of nest. The
Ravens did not go to the nest while I was in the vicinity
but flew about croaking or perched on cliffs. Once one
perched on a bracket of sea-pinks growing on a sheer face
of cliff. When taking off bird gave a little spring and
swooped down on bent wings. Often they glided about the
cliff without a wing-beat and often Herring Gulls stooped
at them. The Ravens avoided these attacks with ease, just
flicking out of the path of the gull. The Ravens themselves
stooped at the Fulmars often as they glided about the
cliffs. One Raven drank from a little pool halfway up the
cliffs, its action similar to that of a crouching hen.

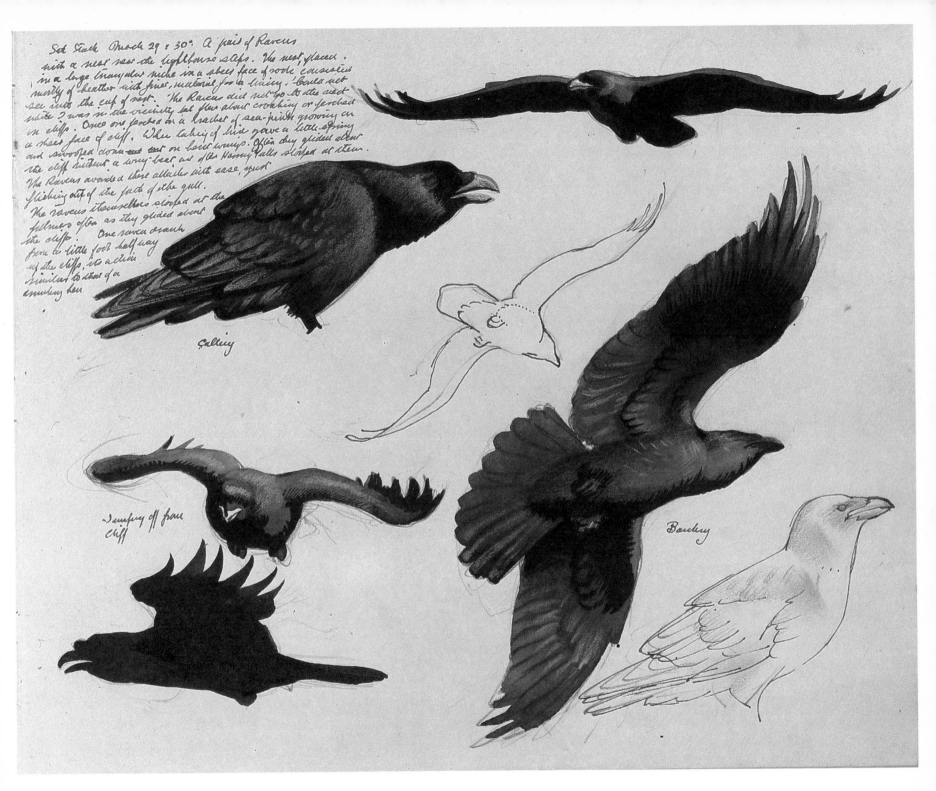

Soft Stack March 29 & 30th A pair of Ravens
with a nest near the lighthouse steps. The nest placed
in a large triangular niche in a sheer face of rock consisted
mostly of heather with finer material for a lining. Could not
see into the cup of nest. The Ravens did not go to the nest
while I was in the vicinity but flew about croaking or perched
in cliffs. Once one perched in a heather of sea-pink growing on
a sheer face of cliff. When taking of this gave a little spring
and swooped down out on bent wings. Often they glided about
the cliff without a wing-beat as the Herring Falls stooped at them.
The Ravens avoided these attacks with ease, just
flicking out of the path of the gull.
The ravens themselves stooped at the
fulmars often as they glided about
the cliff.   One raven crank
from a little foot half way
up the cliffs, its action
similar to those of a
smutting hen

Calling

Dropping off from
cliff

Banking

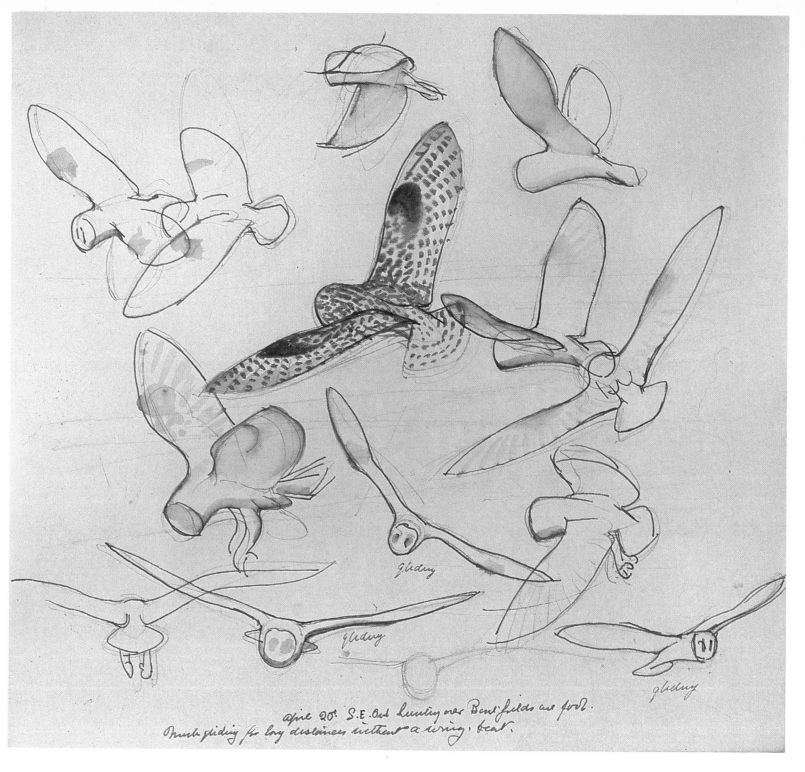

April 20. S.E. Owl hunting over Bont fields are food.

Much gliding for long distances without a wing, beat.

70 Short-eared Owl *Asio flammeus*, Bont Farm, April 20th (? year).

Short-eared Owl hunting over Bont fields and pool. Much gliding for long distances without a wing beat.

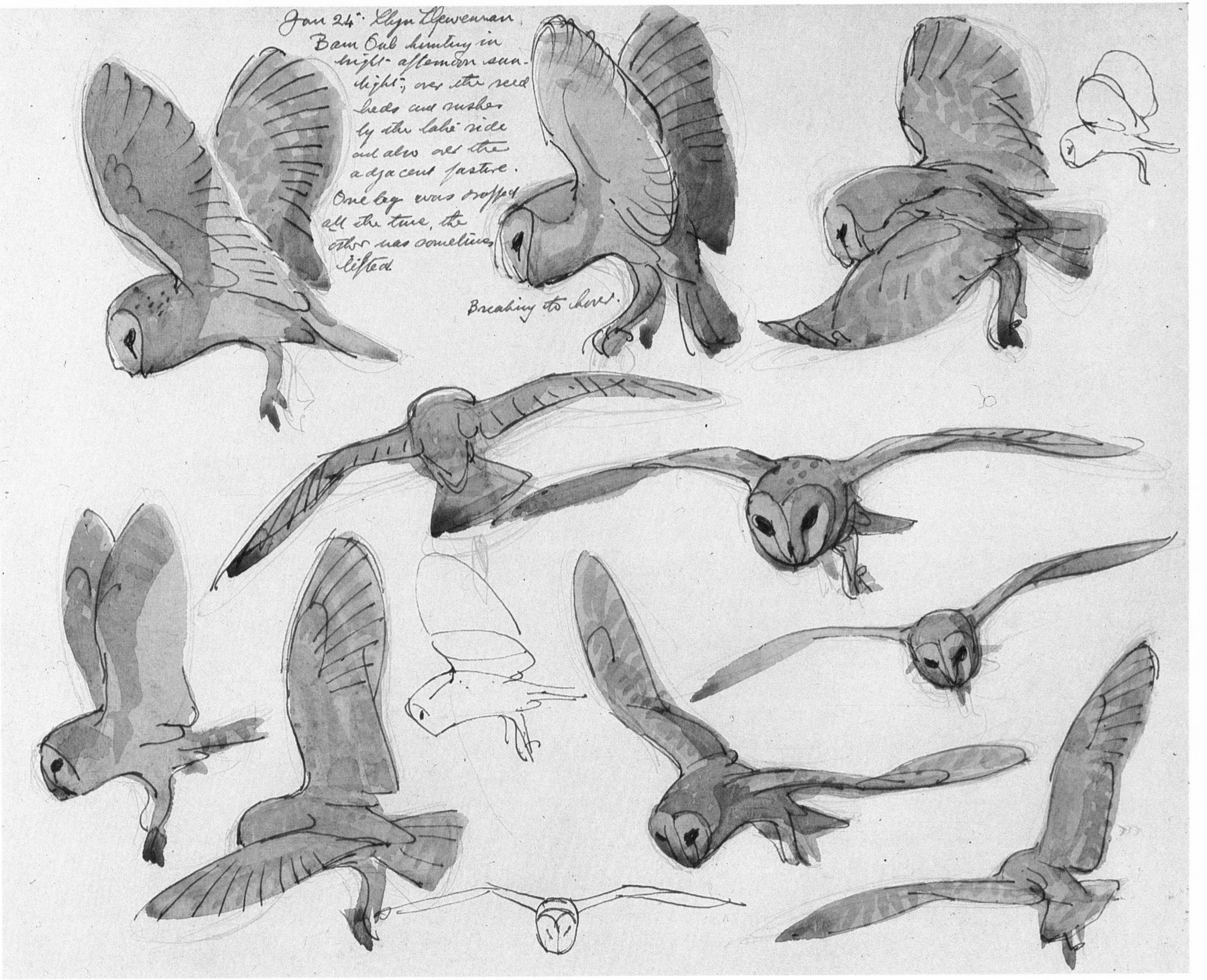
Jan 24th Llyn Llywenan
Barn Owl hunting in bright afternoon sun-light; over the reed beds and rushes by the lake side and also over the adjacent pasture. One leg was dropped all the time, the other was sometimes lifted.
Breaking to hover.

71 Barn Owl *Tyto alba*, Llyn Llywenan, January 24th 1956

Barn Owl hunting in bright afternoon sun-light, over the reed beds and rushes by the lake-side and also over the adjacent pasture. One leg was dropped all the time, the other was sometimes lifted.

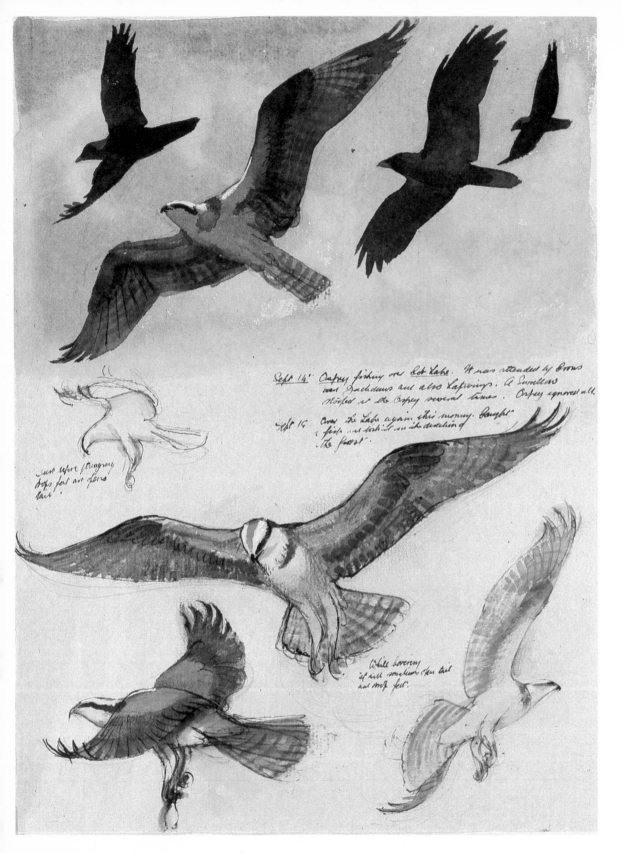

72 Osprey *Pandion haliaëtus*, Cob Lake, September 14th 1969.

It was attended by Crows and Jackdaws and also Lapwings. A Swallow swooped at the Osprey several times. Osprey ignored all.

September 15th. Over the Lake again this morning. Caught a fish and took it in the direction of the forest.

Just before plunging drops feet and opens tail.

While hovering it will sometimes open tail and drop feet.

73 Osprey *Pandion haliaëtus*, Cob Lake, September 14th 1969.

When an Osprey visited Cob Lake, not far from Tunnicliffe's house, he made the most of his chance to draw a bird that rarely came his way. This sketchbook contains several pages of vigorous flight studies. As with the Kestrel (**64**) and Barn Owl (**65**) Tunnicliffe made a series of drawings showing the bird's hunting action. His annotations on the Osprey describe each stage of the steep plunge into the lake after fish.

Osprey almost hovering over the lake accompanied by Crows and Jackdaws and also by Lapwings. Osprey ignored all of them, and was intent on fishing.

Tipping up after sighting a fish. At the beginning stage the legs are dropped as if in readiness for the strike.

Diving down.

Coming out of an unsuccessful stoop possibly because the water was too shallow for a plunge.

Successful plunge causes a big splash. Osprey came out with a fish about nine inches long. This was grasped by its tail in the left foot.

As the fish was small it was carried in one foot, by the tail, until the bird was out of sight beyond the trees of the forest.

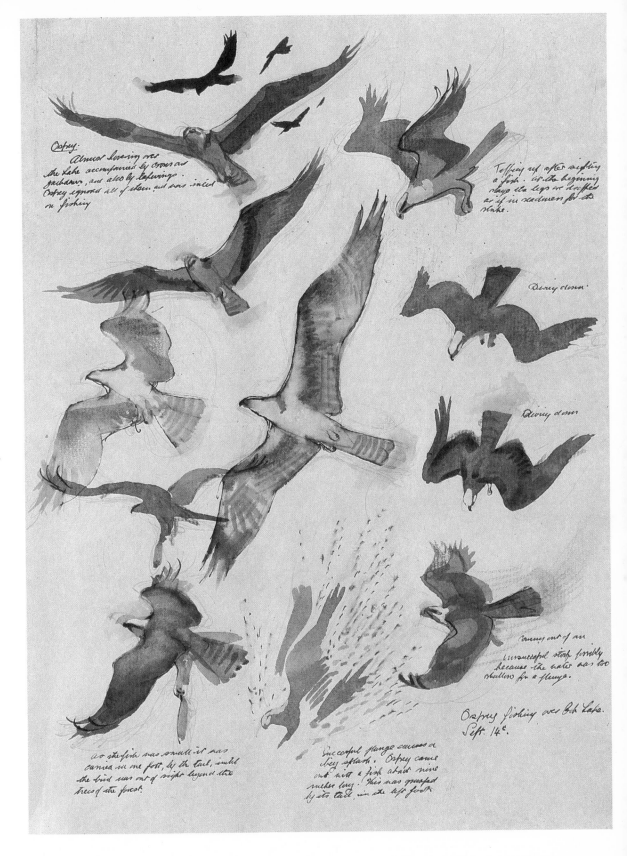

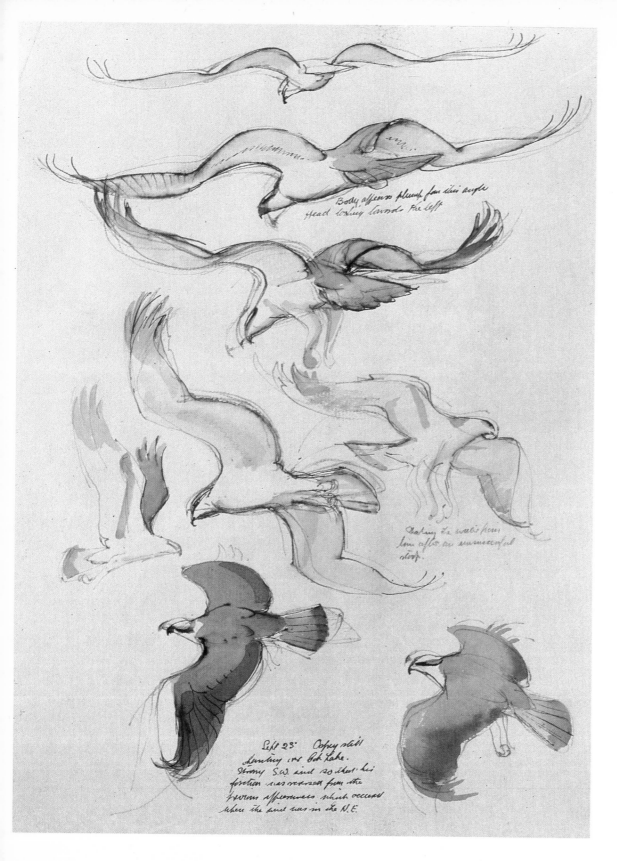

74 Osprey *Pandion haliaëtus*, Cob Lake, September 23rd 1969.

Osprey still hunting over Cob Lake. Strong S.W. wind so that his position was reversed from the previous appearances which occurred when the wind was in the N.E.

On the second drawing from the top, Tunnicliffe notes that the Osprey's *body appears plump from this angle. Head looking towards the left.*

Further down the bird is seen *shaking the water from him after an unsuccessful stoop.*

Other behaviour

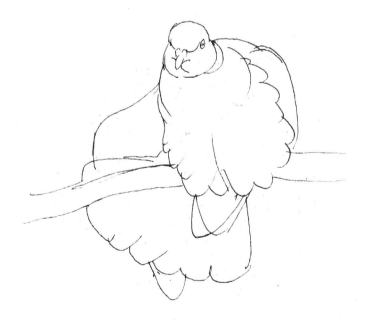

The bird watcher who takes time to *watch* and is not content merely to tick species seen and move on, is rewarded with many fascinating insights into the life of birds. Tunnicliffe was a deeply interested and knowledgeable bird watcher who collected observations rather than names, and filled his sketchbooks with notes and drawings of any aspect of bird life which caught his eye and in which he could see pictorial possibilities. There are scores of drawings for example of birds preening and going through the many actions connected with basic behaviour, such as scratching, stretching, shaking and bathing. The page with several studies of a preening Woodpigeon (**78**) shows Tunnicliffe drawing with the simplest of pen lines and in doing so revealing a sculptor's feeling for form as well as a complete understanding of the structure underlying the softly rounded masses of the pigeon's feathers.

Tunnicliffe's account of a group of Rooks and Jackdaws bathing (**76**), accompanied by a few crisp pen sketches, describes a scene which obviously gave him the greatest pleasure. His final sentences indicate that he was already seeing a picture in his mind. "Wonderful purple sheen on Rooks in the bright sun. Looked fine perched among the yellow leaves of sallow."

There are studies of birds in the rain and in the wind, or trying to shelter from such conditions, when their whole shape seems to change completely, making them look quite different from their usual appearance.

The interaction of birds, in courtship or in combat, provides marvellous material for the artist. I remember a striking painting by Tunnicliffe of drake Shelducks—one seeing off the other in a flurry of black, white and chestnut wings. Included here are two pages with records of birds fighting. The first, of two Curlew (**80**), sketched in a sequence of drawings made with great economy of line and colour, has notes which are equally brief but to the point. They provide an entirely adequate account of an encounter which could be recalled and re-created later in visual terms. The second record of birds fighting is of two Herons (**81**)—a sketch which was certainly used later for a painting.

The cock Blackbird (**82**), indulging in anting, shows an aspect of bird behaviour which, although it has attracted a good deal of attention, is still imperfectly understood. Many passerine species rub ants along their wing feathers or allow ants to swarm over them as they spreadeagle themselves by the ants' nest. The formic acid in the ants, released either by the bird's action of wiping or by the ants spraying it over the intruder at the nest, may help to rid the bird of parasites or have some other beneficial effect on the bird's feathers. It is most often seen in summer, particularly when ants are swarming. Among the notes to the drawings of the Green Woodpeckers (**37**) is the comment that Starlings were also watched anting. This was three days after the Blackbird and near the same place.

75 Barn Owl *Tyto alba* and Magpie *Pica pica*, Llanfaelog, February 13th 1957.

Barn Owl flying and hunting at noon. Came to rest on a wall. Magpie also flew to the wall and rested four feet from owl. Magpie bounced up and flew just over owl's head to its other side, then flew back. After this to and fro annoyance, during which the owl turned its head always facing Magpie, the owl flew off. As it hunted the field and hedge it was swooped at several times by Herring Gulls.

Previous page: Woodpigeon *Columba palumbus*

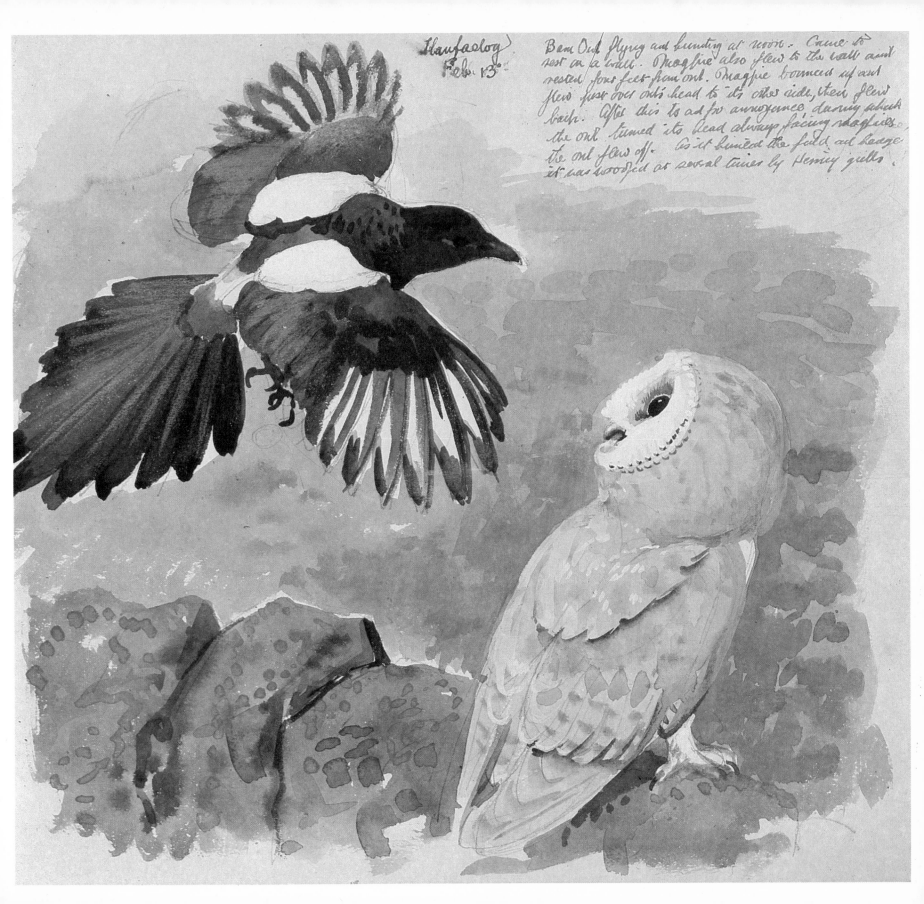

Llanfaelog
Feb. 13th

Barn Owl flying and hunting at noon. Came to
rest on a wall. Magpie also flew to the wall and
rested four feet from owl. Magpie bounced up and
flew just over owl's head to its other side, then flew
back. After this to ad for annoyance, during which
the owl turned its head always facing magpie,
the owl flew off. As it hunted the field and hedge
it was mobbed at several times by Henry gulls.

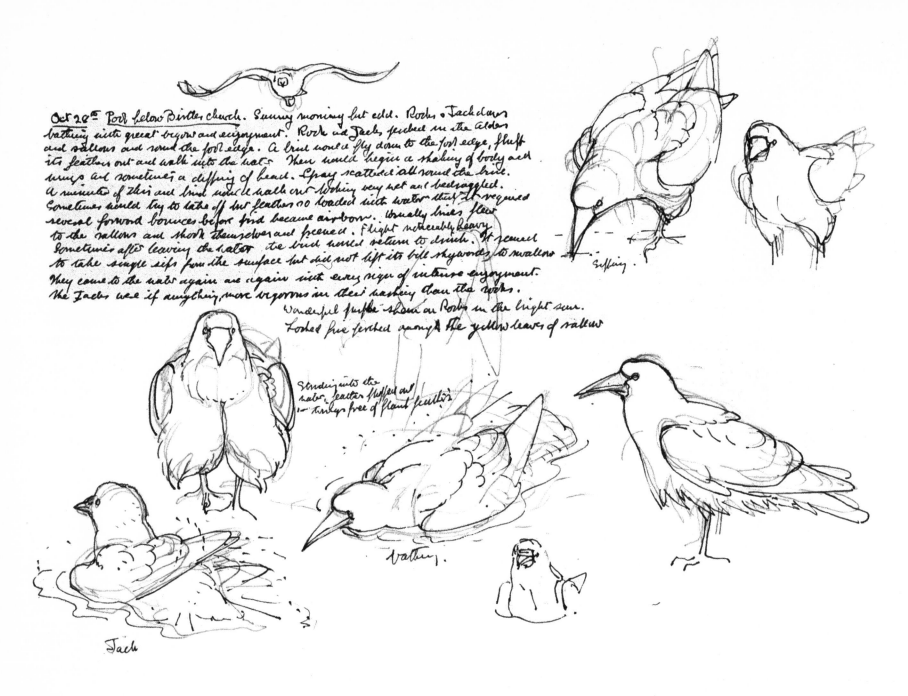

76 Rook *Corvus frugilegus* and Jackdaw *Corvus monedula*, pool below Birtles Church, October 28th 1947.

Sunny morning but cold. Rooks and Jackdaws bathing with great vigour and enjoyment. Rooks and Jacks perched in the Alders and sallows and round the pool edge. A bird would fly down to the pool edge, fluff its feathers out and walk into the water. Then would begin a shaking of body and wings and sometimes a dipping of head. Spray scattered all round the bird. A minute of this and bird would walk out looking very wet and bedraggled. Sometimes would try to take off but feathers so loaded with water that it required several forward bounces before bird became airborne. Usually birds flew to the sallows and shook themselves and preened. Flight noticeably heavy. Sometimes after leaving the water the bird would return to drink. It seemed to take single sips from the surface but did not lift its bill skywards to swallow. They came to the water again and again with every sign of intense enjoyment. The Jacks were if anything, more vigorous in their washing than the Rooks. Wonderful purple sheen on Rooks in the bright sun. Looked fine perched among the yellow leaves of sallow.

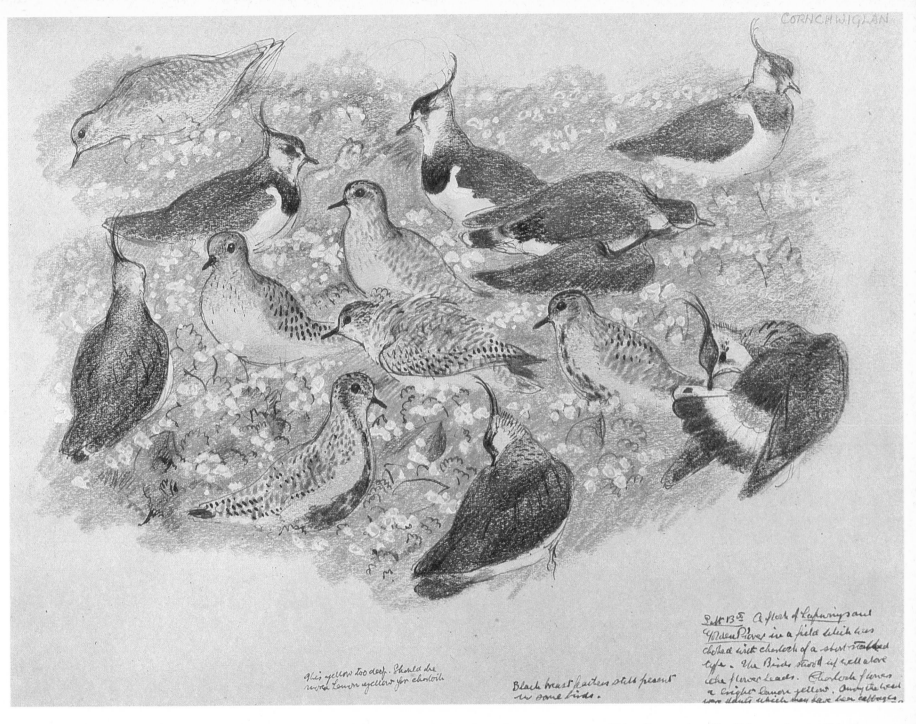

This yellow too deep. Should be more lemon yellow for charlock.

Black breast feathers still present in some birds.

Sept 13ᵗʰ A flock of Lapwings and Golden Plover in a field which was choked with charlock of a short stalked type. The Birds stood up well above the flower heads. Charlock flowers a bright lemon yellow. Among the weeds were plants which may have been cabbages.

77 Lapwing *Vanellus vanellus* and Golden Plover *Charadrius apricarius*, Anglesey, September 13th 1944.

There are a great variety of poses in this lovely drawing: preening, scratching, shaking and feeding.

Tunnicliffe has added a number of annotations, suggesting that he saw this colourful scene as a promising subject for a painting.

A flock of Lapwings and Golden Plover in a field which was choked with charlock of a short stalked type. The birds stood up well above the flower heads. Charlock flowers a bright lemon yellow. Among the weeds were plants which may have been cabbages.

This yellow too deep. Should be more lemon yellow for charlock.

Black breast feathers still present in some birds. (Golden Plover.)

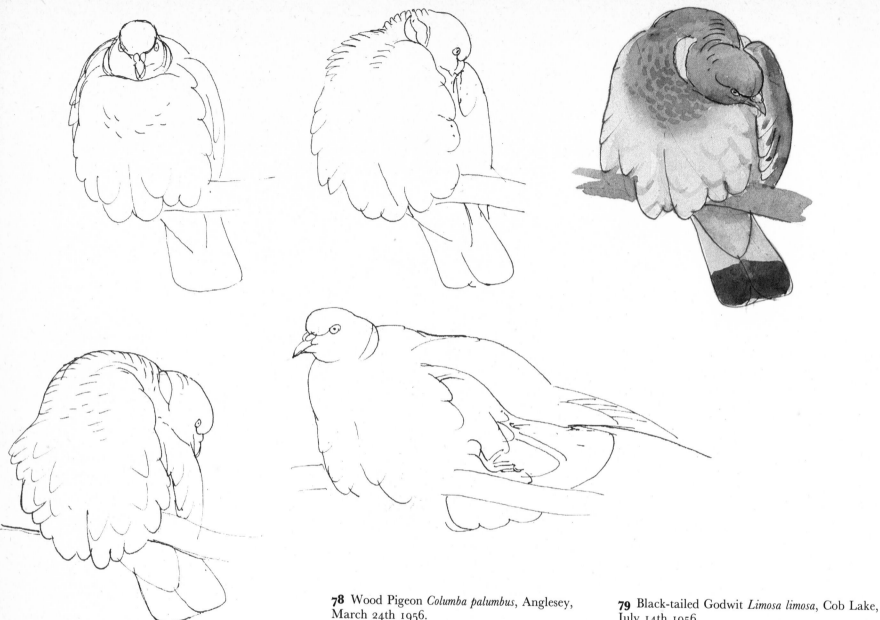

78 Wood Pigeon *Columba palumbus*, Anglesey, March 24th 1956.

Fascinating too, are the poses of a bird when it is preening, for the feathers of the whole body are preened either by beak or toe, and to accomplish this the bird twists itself into all sorts of interesting attitudes. As the bird rummages with its beak, you will see first one set of feathers lifted, then another; wings will be half-opened, and flight feathers will each receive careful attention, as also will the tail feathers. Preening is often accompanied by wing, tail, and leg-stretching, actions which result in novel, delectable poses for the pages of your sketch book.

Bird Portraiture.

79 Black-tailed Godwit *Limosa limosa*, Cob Lake, July 14th 1956.

A most beautifully marked male.

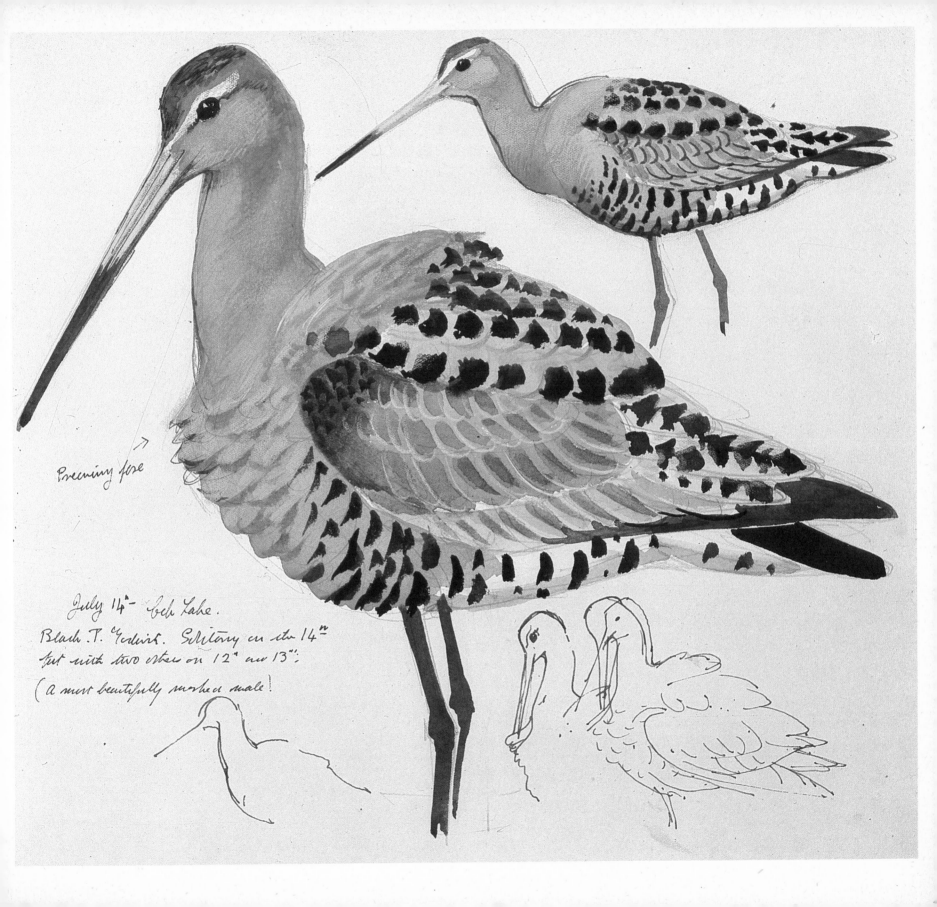

Preening pose

July 14th - Loch Lake.
Black T. Godwit. Solitary on the 14"
but with two others on 12" and 13".
(a most beautifully marked male!)

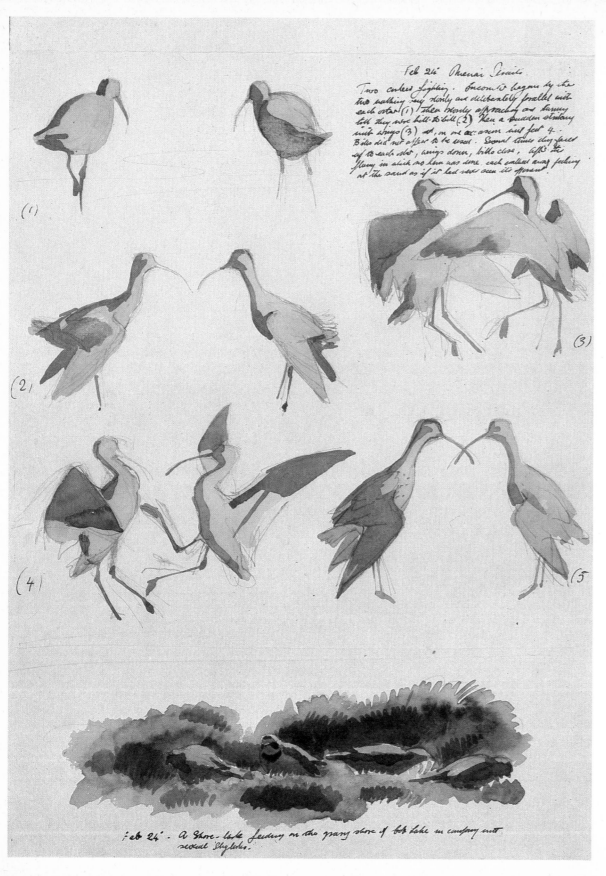

Feb 24ᵗʰ Menai Straits.

Two curlews fighting. Encounter began by the two walking very slowly and deliberately parallel with each other (1). then slowly approaching as turning till they were bill-to-bill (2). Then a sudden striking with wings (3) and, on one occasion with feet 4. Bills did not appear to be used. Several times they faced up to each other, wings down, bills close, left its flurry in which no harm was done, each walked away pecking at the sand as if it had never seen its opponent.

(1)

(2)

(3)

(4)

(5)

Feb 24ᵗʰ. A Shore-lark feeding on the grassy shore of Cob Lake in company with several Skylarks.

80 Curlew *Numenius arquata*, Menai Straits, February 24th 1966.

Two Curlew fighting. Encounter began by the two walking very slowly and deliberately parallel with each other (1). Then slowly approaching and turning till they were bill-to-bill (2). Then a sudden striking with wings (3) and, on one occasion, with feet (4). Bills did not appear to be used. Several times they faced up to each other, wings down, bills close (5). After this flurry in which no harm was done each walked away pecking at the sand as if it had never seen its opponent.

Below, Shorelark *Eremophila alpestris* and Skylark *Alauda arvensis*.

A Shore-lark feeding on the grassy shore of Cob Lake in company with several Skylarks.

81 Heron *Ardea cinerea*, Cob Lake, June 9th 1948.

No notes accompany this spirited sketch of two adult Herons fighting and posturing. Herons, often seen standing gaunt and still, can be surprisingly agile and active and their fights spectacularly energetic.

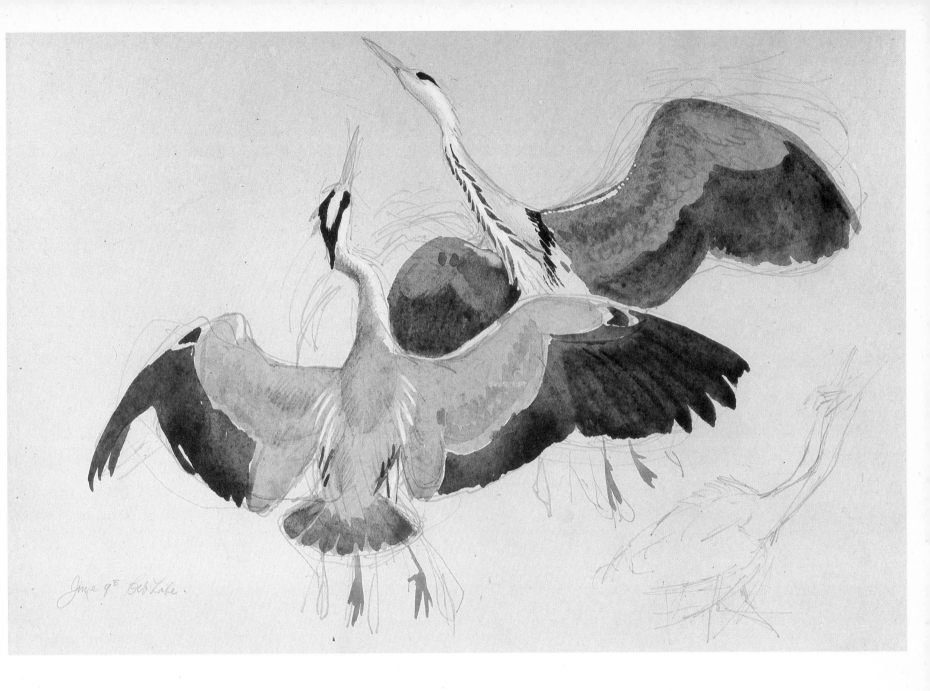

June 9th Ebb Lake.

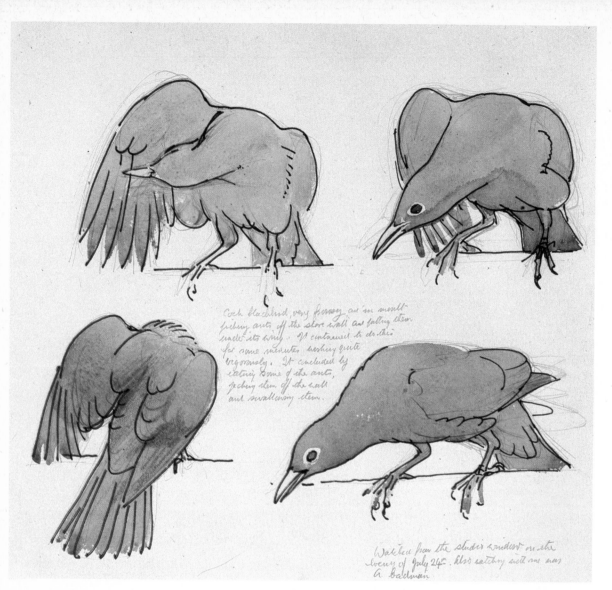

Cock Blackbird, very frowsy and in moult picking ants off the shore wall and putting them under its wing. It continued to do this for some minutes working quite vigorously. It concluded by eating some of the ants, pecking them off the wall and swallowing them.

Watched from the studio window in the evening of July 24th. Also watching with me was A. Cadman

82 Blackbird *Turdus merula*, Shorelands, evening of July 24th 1958.

An anting Blackbird watched from the house. It is likely that the bird was wiping the ants along its feathers when "putting them under its wing", thereby leaving formic acid where it might help to rid the bird of parasites.

Cock Blackbird, very frowsy and in moult, picking ants off the shore wall and putting them under its wing. It continued to do this for some minutes working quite vigorously. It concluded by eating some of the ants, pecking them off the wall and swallowing them.

83 Mistle Thrush *Turdus viscivorus*, Beach Terrace, March 9th 1957.

A nest-building Mistle Thrush tugging at a derelict aerial wire on the roof of Beach Terrace. It persisted for some minutes and at last flew away with some of the wire covering (cotton) in its bill.

Below, a pencil sketch of two drakes, Goldeneye *Bucephala clangula*.

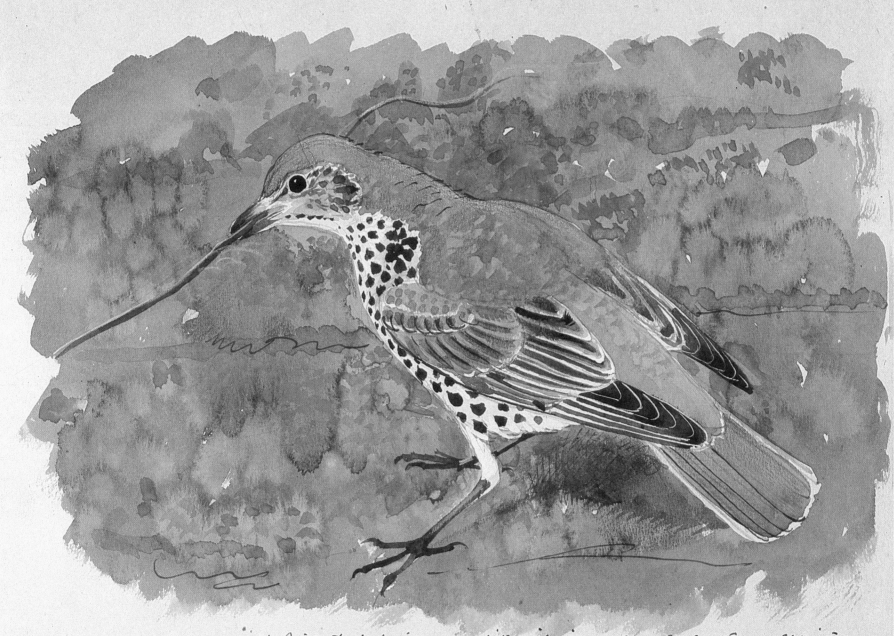

March 9th. A nest-building Mistle-thrush tugging at a "derelict" aerial wire on the roof of Beech Terrace. It persisted for some minutes and at last flew away with some of the wire coating (cotton) in its bill.

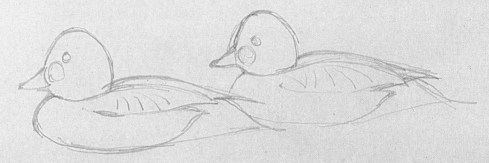

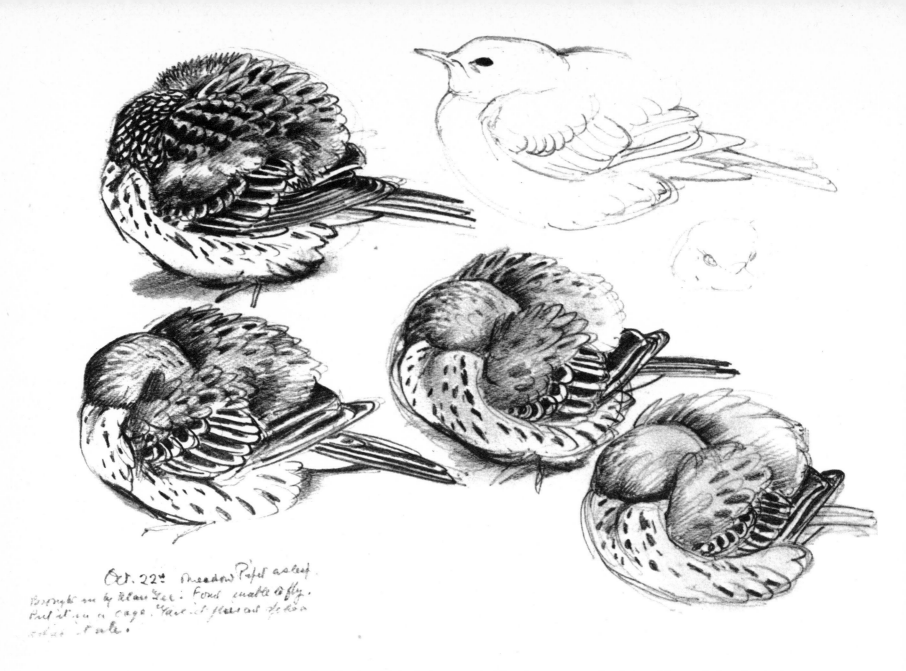

Oct. 22nd Meadow Pipit asleep.
Brought in by Alan Gee. Found unable to fly.
Put it in a cage. Gave it flies and spiders
which it ate.

84 Meadow Pipit *Anthus pratensis*, Shorelands, October 22nd 1950.

When Tunnicliffe had the chance to draw direct from the living model at length, and at close quarters, he made some exquisite drawings. (See also numbers **18**, **30** and **122**.)

Meadow Pipit asleep. Brought in by Alan Gee. Found unable to fly. Put in a cage. Gave it flies and spiders which it ate.

85 Smew *Mergus albellus*, Cob Lake, February 10th 1954.

A series of studies, in wash and opaque white on grey paper, of a drake Smew in a variety of poses—done in the studio from field sketches and from memory.

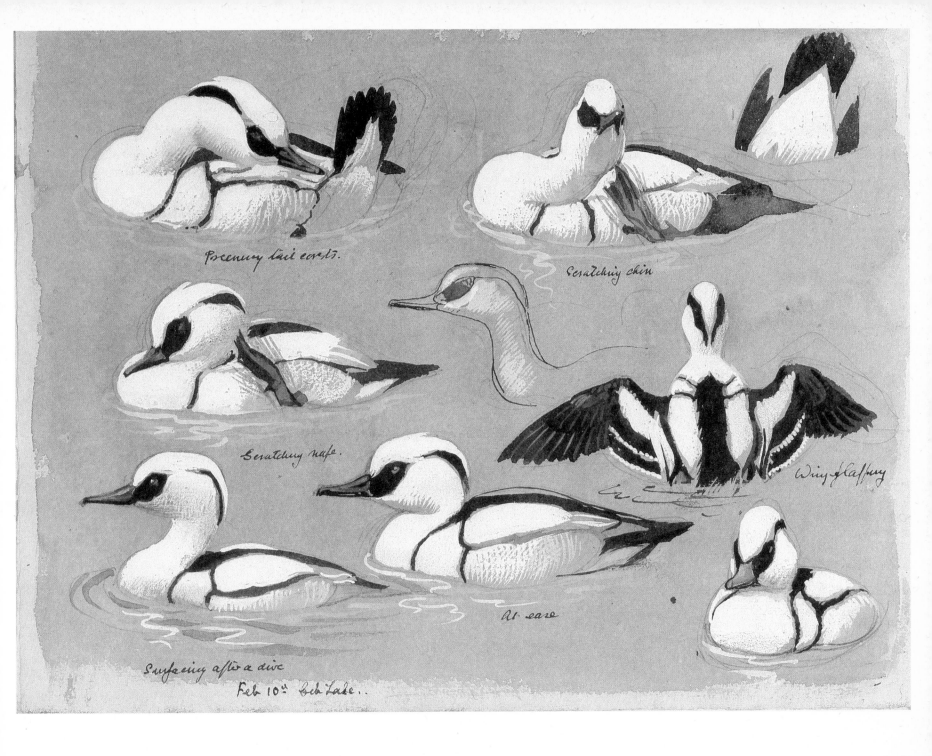

Preening tail coverts.

Scratching chin

Scratching nape.

Wing flapping

Surfacing after a dive
Feb 10ᵗʰ Loch Lake.

At ease

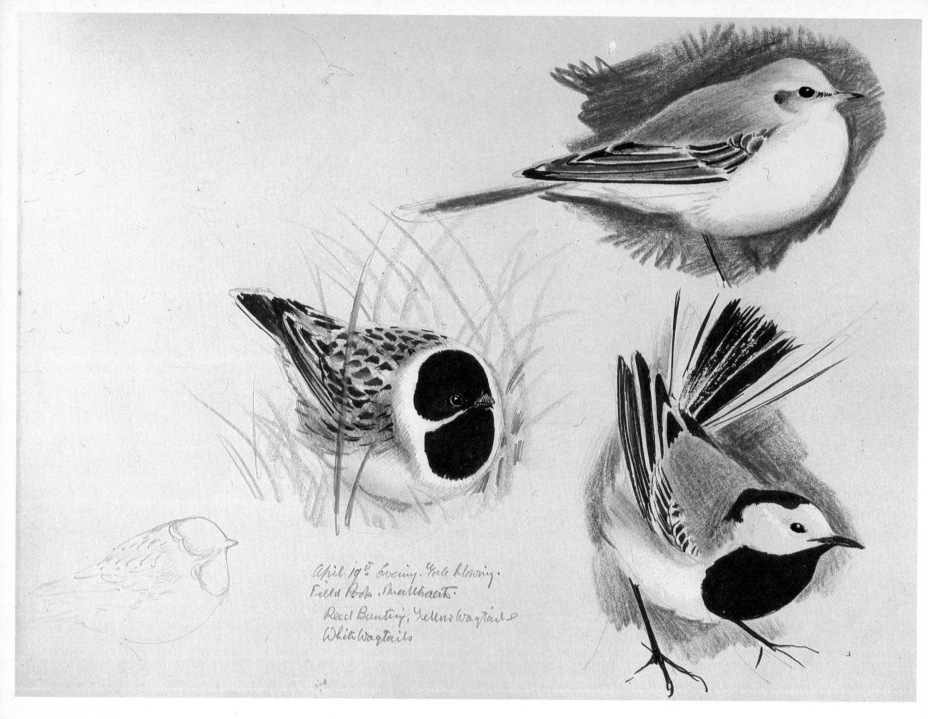

In the illustration, handwritten notes read:

April 19ᵗʰ Evening Gale blowing.
Field Pools Malltraeth.
Reed Bunting, Yellow Wagtail ♀
White Wagtails

86 Yellow Wagtail *Motacilla flava*, (top) Reed Bunting *Emberiza schoeniclus*, (left) and White Wagtail *Motacilla alba alba*, (right), Field Pools, Malltraeth, evening of 19th April 1948.

It was while we were watching the bird traffic that the glasses rested upon a spot of bright yellow at the edge of the pool. I saw that it was a cock Yellow Wagtail, very

exquisite and vivid even as he huddled in the earth bank. Later he moved up on the grass and hunted with his White cousins, and it was interesting to note how much smaller he was when compared with them. Gusts blew their feathers awry, and tails were disarranged, but they continued their quest for food among the tumps of grass growing from the swamp. With them were Meadow-pipits, and then W. discovered the Reed-buntings—two of

them, one a young cock bird, the other an adult cock in the most flawless plumage I have ever seen on any bird. He was unbelievably smart and handsome and no words could truly convey the effect of his black head and bib against his white collar and striped back.

Shorelands Summer Diary.

Picture making

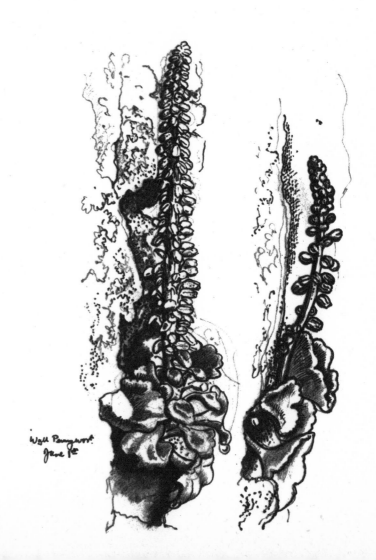

Wall Pennywort
Jane P=

In a BBC television interview in October 1976, Tunnicliffe talked about sketching birds: ". . . you must start with the live bird to get life into your drawings . . . get a sketchbook out and get as much of a live bird in it as you possibly can, and when he flies away from you, you go home and you have another sketchbook where you try to memorise what you've seen." On another occasion he referred to the importance of getting ". . . the essence of the bird within its own surroundings and its own environment." Both of these statements are characteristic of his approach to drawing and painting birds, with the emphasis on studying the living bird.

Tunnicliffe based his watercolour paintings very closely on field observations and used his sketchbooks extensively for ideas, designs and poses. In many cases the finished painting was very close to the original sketch although much fresh thought was given to the final composition—an aspect of picture making which Tunnicliffe considered tremendously important—and to what decorative elements could be introduced or emphasised. When looking through the sketches and making a selection for this book, I kept finding the source of paintings I had seen, perhaps at a Royal Academy Summer Exhibition. Tracing the development of a picture throws light on the way Tunnicliffe worked and this process is shown in the series of studies of a Whooper Swan bathing (numbers **92**—**95**). In February 1954 Tunnicliffe sketched Whooper Swans bathing in Cob Lake and, with the sketches beside him, made a further colour drawing in the studio. Six years later, when preparing his paintings for the Royal Academy, he turned up those sketches and re-worked them. Small drawings, done freely in colour, established the main composition before a full size cartoon was made on thin tracing paper. He described this stage as ". . . where all the scheming is done." Once settled, the drawing could be transferred to the watercolour paper without further working. He explained ". . . watercolour paper does not take kindly to designing and that sort of thing." First, the back of the tracing paper was scribbled over with soft pencil and then the drawing was traced onto the watercolour paper with a hard pencil, leaving a clean outline ready for the washes with which he would build up the painting. The result was a picture full of action and, with the splashes patterning the water, splendidly decorative as well.

Tunnicliffe also made drawings of habitats and the details of the immediate environment of birds—including trees, flowers, rocks and water textures—essential references for picture making (**96–102**). Two pages (**104** and **105**) from different sketchbooks, thirteen years apart, show the richness of bird life around Tunnicliffe's home. There were few days when he did not look to see what there was on Cob Lake. Occasionally he was rewarded with the unexpected (**106–109**). He said: "The estuary is a continual source of subject matter and the variety is also tremendous. I shall never exhaust its possibilities."

Previous page: Wall Pennywort *Umbilicus rupestris*

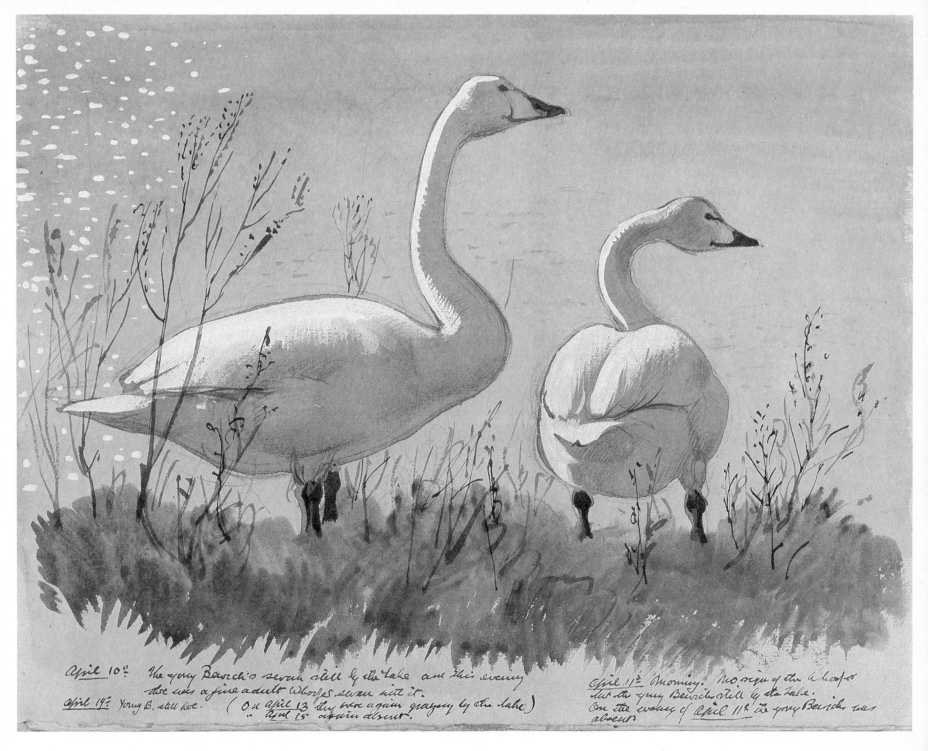

87 Whooper Swan *Cygnus cygnus*, left, and Bewick's Swan *Cygnus bewickii*, Cob Lake, April 10th 1954.

The young Bewick's swan still by the lake and this evening there was a fine adult Whooper swan with it.

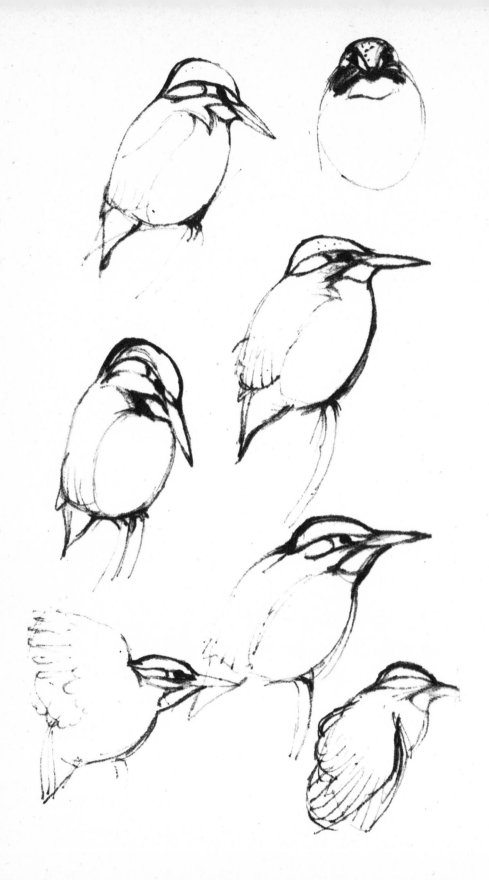

88 and **89** Kingfisher *Alcedo atthis*, Redesmere, August 12th 1944.

These studies of a Kingfisher are sketches from life, made in a field sketchbook. On the right is a page from the studio sketchbook where the same field notes were worked-up into more finished drawings in colour. Notes were added referring to reflected light from the water and the behaviour of the bird. Such drawings, made immediately on return home while the memory is still clear, are invaluable to the artist and Tunnicliffe used this method of recording in two sketchbooks—one in the field and one in the studio—over a long period. The result is many sketchbooks of beautifully finished coloured drawings which retain the freshness of recent observation.

Kingfisher perched in an alder bush, in shadow. Light on breast reflected from the water. No direct light on back and wings but when the back and rump was visible the electric blue-green flashed in the shade. Bird made several plunges and caught fish. Also stretched wings above back and, singly, downwards and backwards.

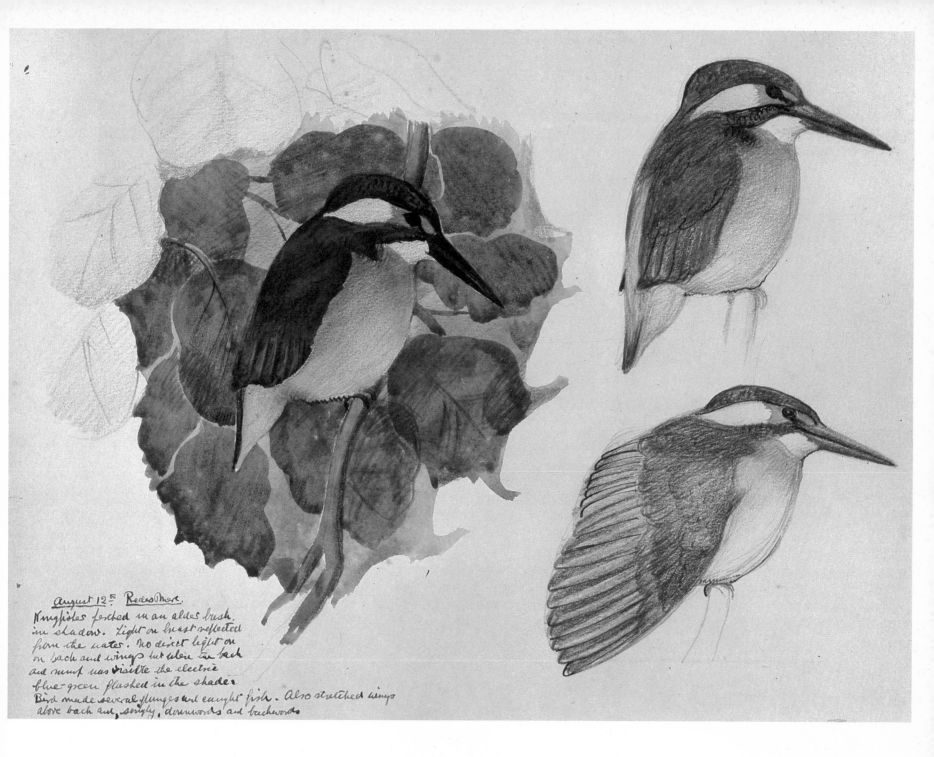

August 12th. Redesmere.
Kingfisher perched in an alder bush,
in shadow. Light on breast reflected
from the water. No direct light on
on back and wings but when the back
and rump was visible the electric
blue-green flashed in the shade.
Bird made several plunges and caught fish. Also stretched wings
above back and, singly, downwards and backwards

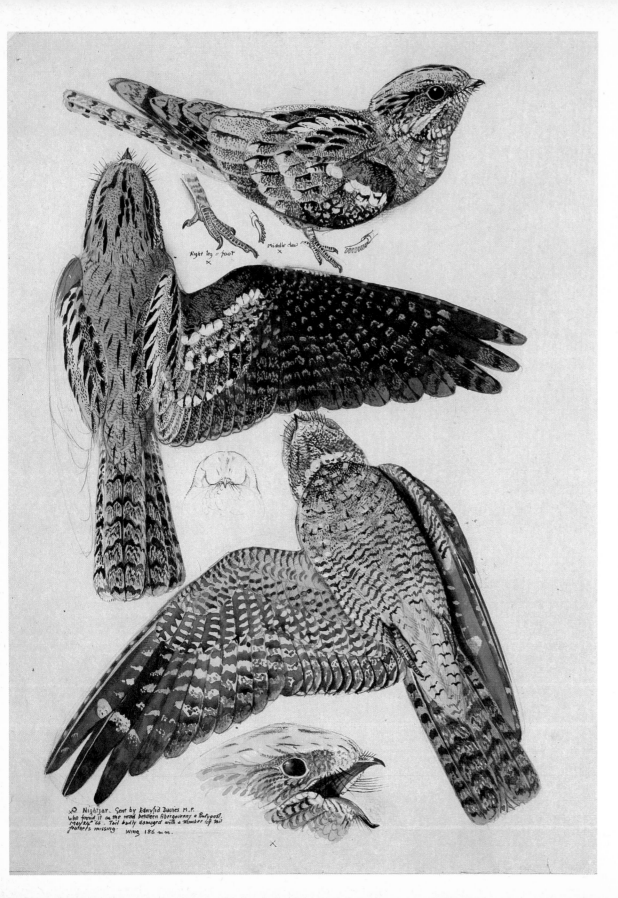

90 Nightjar *Caprimulgus europaeus*, North Wales, May 24th 1966.

Measured drawing of a female Nightjar sent to Tunnicliffe by Ednyfed Davies M.P. who had found it on the road between Abergavenny and Pontypool. The tail was badly damaged with a number of tail feathers missing. The wing measured 186 mm.

Over a period of forty years Tunnicliffe made a unique series of over 350 drawings of dead birds and mammals, each accurately measured to exact life size. They were carried out in a variety of media to achieve amazingly accurate renderings of feather texture: the soft dense whiteness of a Gannet; the rich, glossy black of a Chough, or, as in this example, the dry looking, broken and complex pattern of a Nightjar's plumage. His instinctive feel for composition is evident in the way the various studies are placed on the sheet, with each position of the bird carefully arranged to show the different parts to best advantage.

91 Nightjar *Caprimulgus europaeus*, Bodorgan, June 2nd 1944.

Nightjars sit tight on their eggs, relying on their remarkable camouflage for protection. They can be approached closely, if you know just where to look, and this is one of four drawings made from a distance of only five feet. Tunnicliffe described the nest site on another page of the sketchbook.

On a grass covered rocky outcrop on poor pasture with bracken sprays growing. In close proximity to bird was an old grey stump of gorse lying on ground; stalks of dead bracken; several new sprays of bracken. The nest was made on grass. Two eggs in nest.

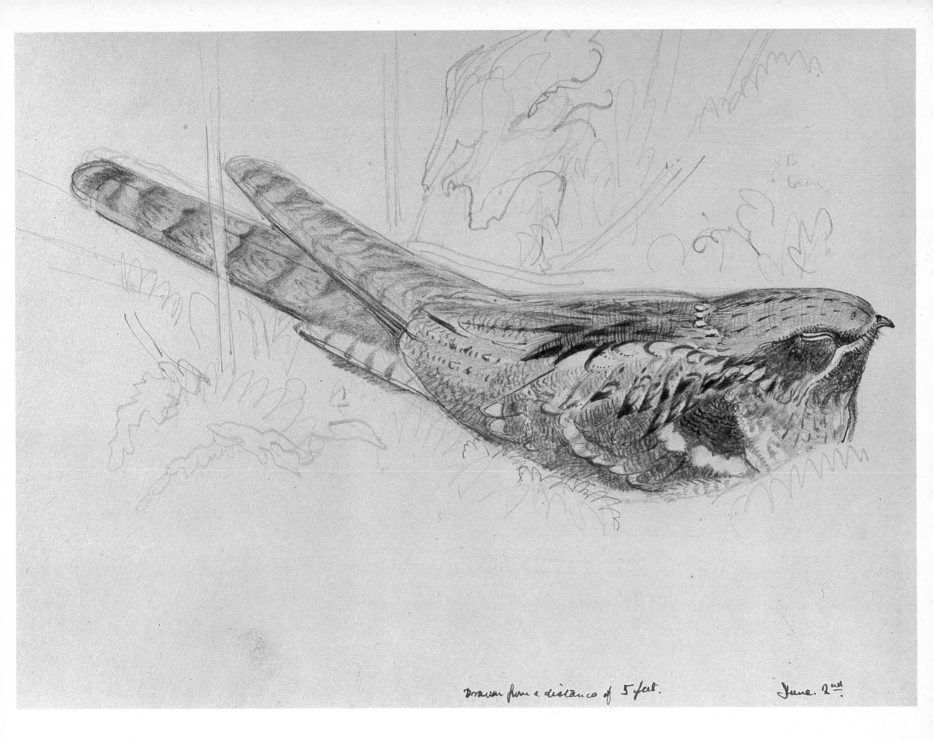

Drawn from a distance of 5 feet.   June. 2nd.

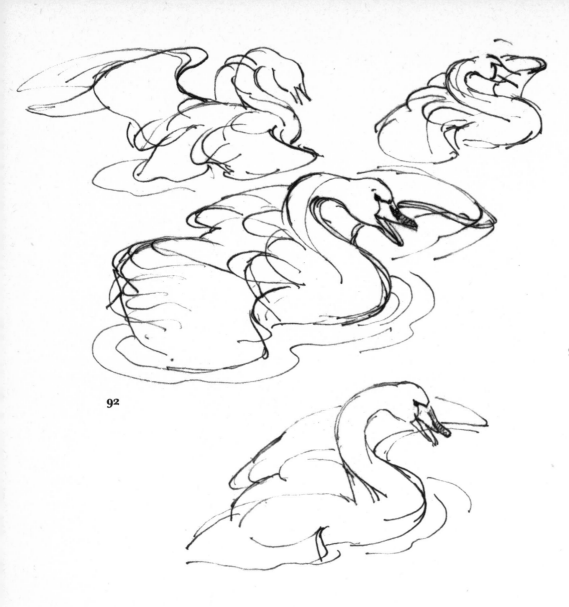

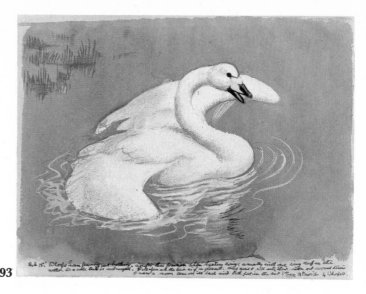

93

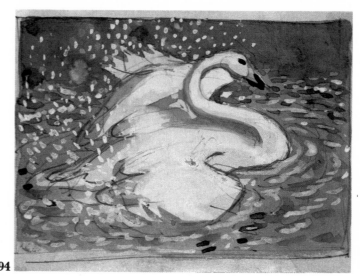

94

92–95 Whooper Swan *Cygnus cygnus*, Cob Lake, February 15th 1954.

Three preliminary studies for the painting, reproduced opposite, of a bathing Whooper Swan.

92 Some of the original field sketches in pencil.

93 Watercolour drawing (greatly reduced) drawn in the studio on return home. The following notes were added before the memory faded.

Whooper Swan preening and bathing. Adopts this position when beating wings usually with one wing deep in the water. As a rule tail is submerged. Bill open all the time as if in pleasure. They would roll onto their sides and several times I saw a swan turn on its back with both feet in the air.

94 Tunnicliffe invariably made a small sketch (reproduced here the same size as the original) establishing the main composition and colour scheme. He then made a full size cartoon on thin paper where the drawing would be worked out in detail before being transferred to the watercolour paper.

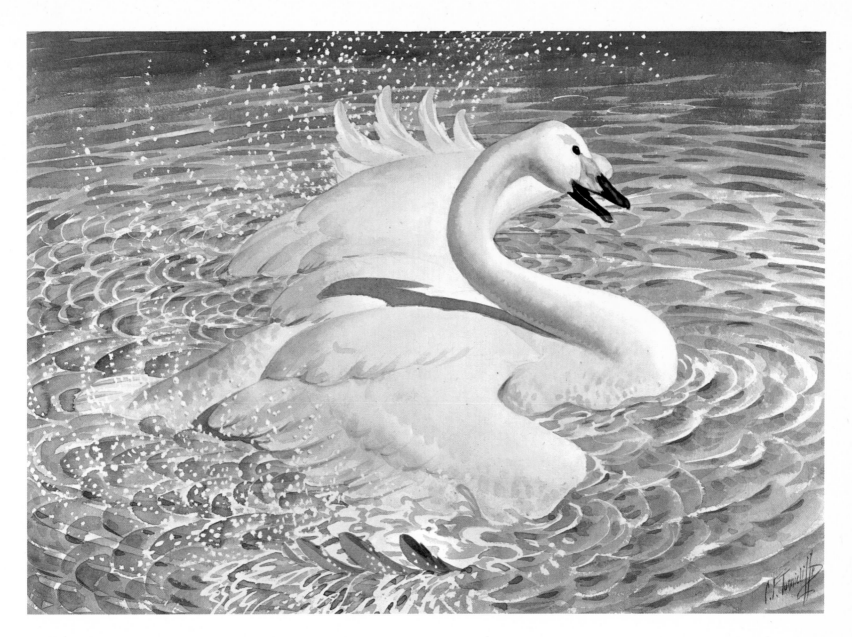

95 The painting, *Whooper Bathing*, exhibited in the
Royal Academy in 1960, was based on the studies
opposite. Tunnicliffe developed and improved the
coloured sketch, taking note of the comments he
wrote at the time. The water surface is broken by
the bird's vigorous movements and splashes,
making a wonderfully decorative surround to the
pure, smooth whiteness of the swan. This painting
demonstrates his mastery of the painting of water.

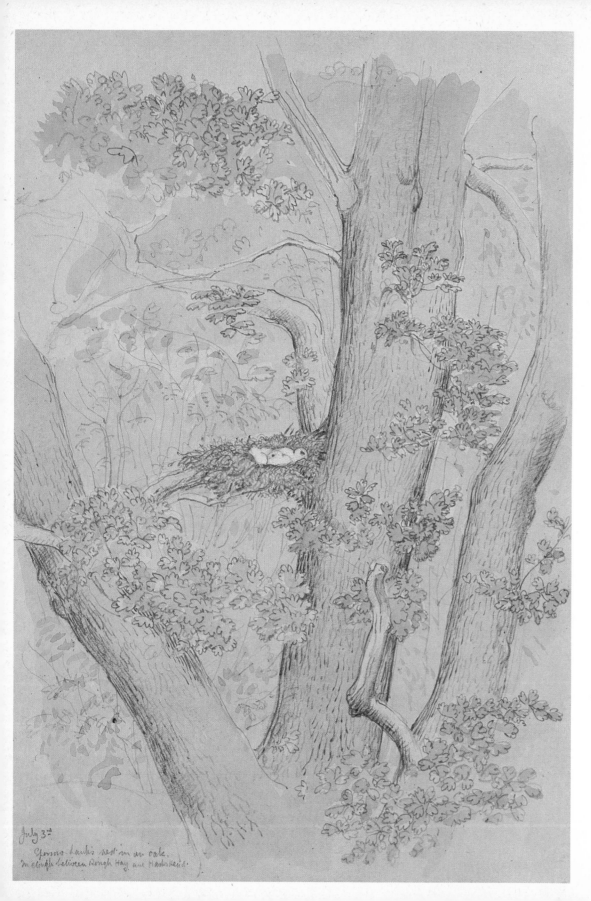

July 3rd

Sparrow-hawk's nest in an oak.
in clough between Rough Hay and Hawks-head.

96 Nest of Sparrowhawk *Accipiter nisus*, in an oak, in clough between Rough Hay and Hawks-head, July 3rd 1947.

Habitat studies such as these are almost as important to the bird artist as drawings of the birds themselves. The Sparrowhawk's nest was one which Tunnicliffe watched over a period and where he made a number of drawings of the young in the nest. The drawing of the Alder stump is typical of the kind of setting that he was searching for to provide a decorative frame or background to his water-bird compositions.

97 Alder stump, with Little Grebe *Podiceps ruficollis*, Redesmere, November 8th 1936.

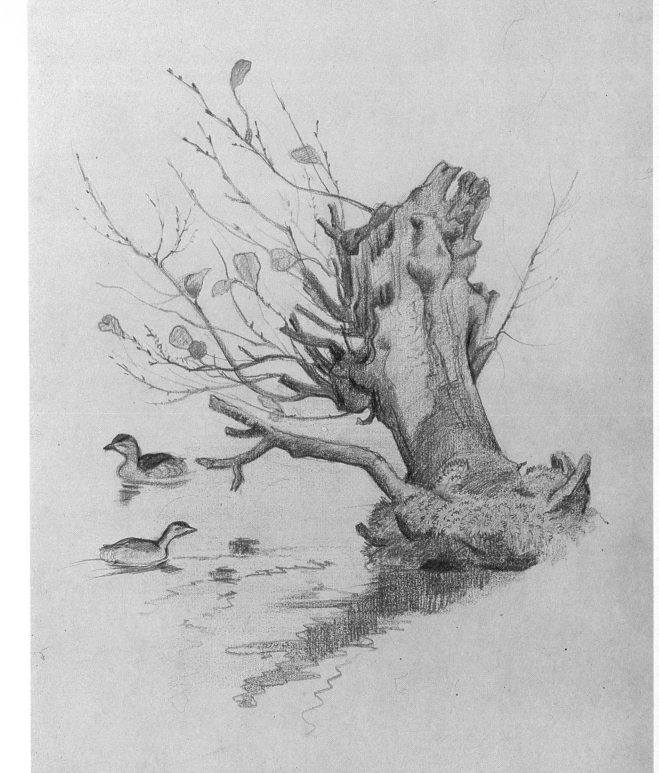

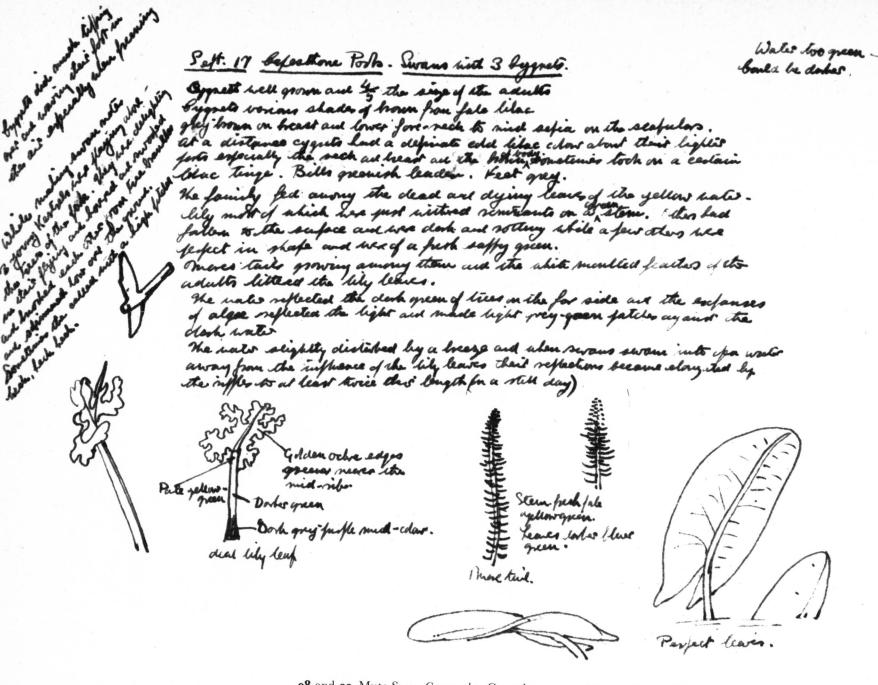

98 and **99** Mute Swan *Cygnus olor*, Capesthorne Pools, September 17th 1945.

A double-spread of notes and studies of a family of Mute Swans. A painting based on this sketch, reproduced on page 56 of *Portrait of a Country Artist*, was exhibited at the Manchester Academy the following year, 1946.

Clearly Tunnicliffe had seen a potential painting in this quiet group feeding amongst the dying leaves of yellow water-lilies, mares-tails and the white, moulted feathers of the adults. His notes are full of information about colours, tones, reflections, the water plants and other details which would all be of the greatest value when re-creating the scene in the studio, perhaps at a much later date.

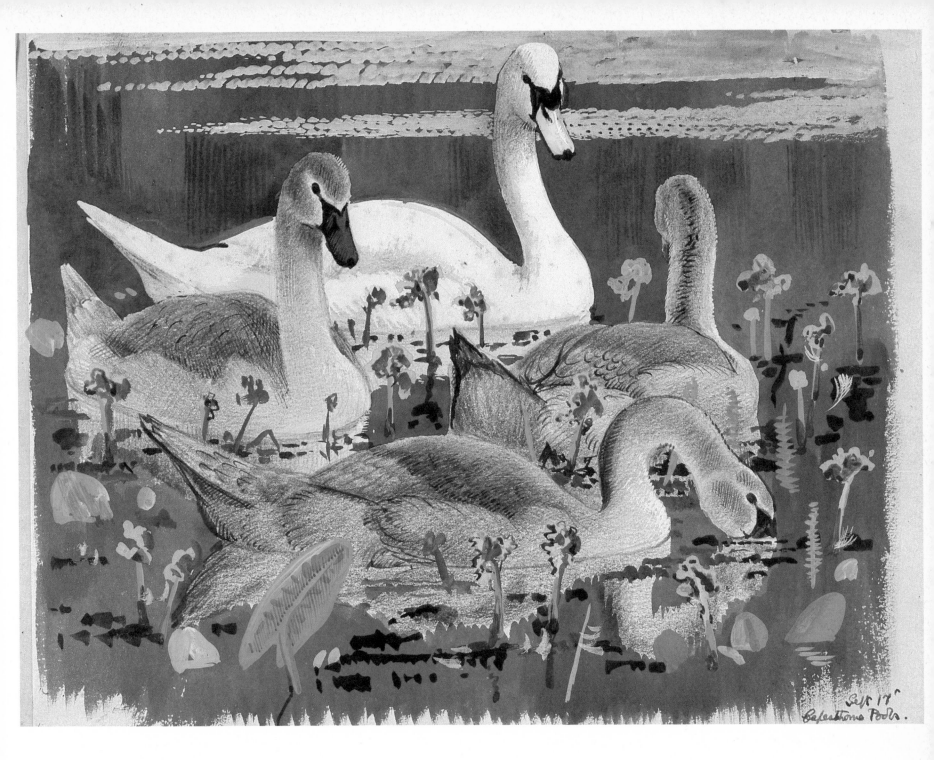

Sept 17
Galesthorpe Pools.

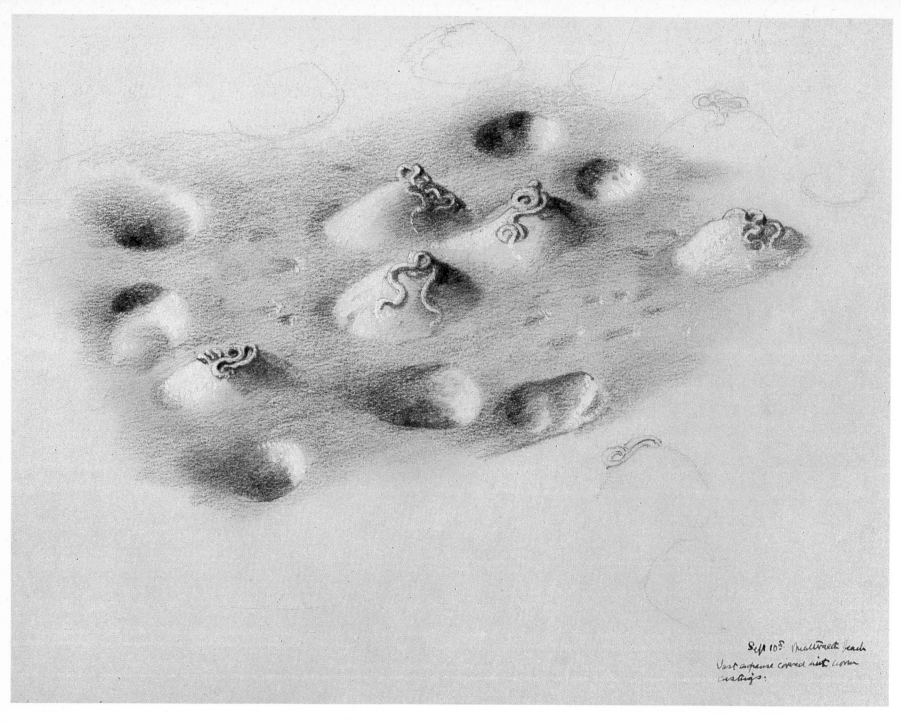

Sept 10ᵗʰ Malltraeth beach
Vast expanse covered with worm
castings:

100 Worm castings on Malltraeth beach,
September 10th 1944.

Scattered through the sketchbooks are delightful
drawings of the immediate surroundings of birds
which might be useful in picture making.
Tunnicliffe undoubtedly saw and enjoyed the
decorative elements in these humble worm casts.

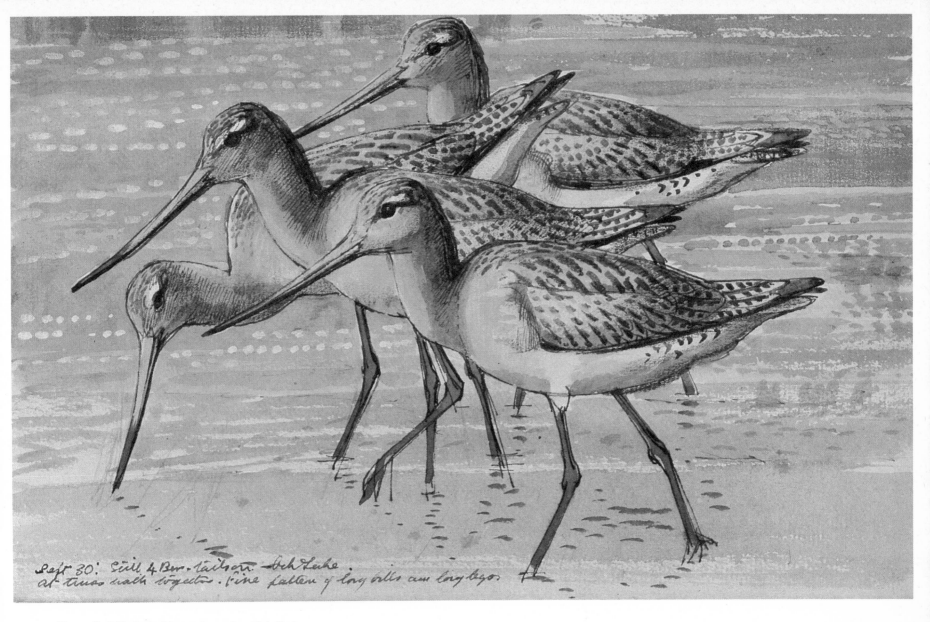

Sept 30: Still 4 Bar-tailed. Och Lake.
at times walk together. Fine pattern of long bills and long legs

101 Bar-tailed Godwit *Limosa lapponica*, Cob Lake,
September 30th 1955.

At all times Tunnicliffe was looking for the
pictorial possibilities in the birds he was watching
and sketching. The note added to this lovely
drawing, done in pen, wash and crayon, indicates
just that.

*At times walk together. Fine pattern of long bills and
long legs.*

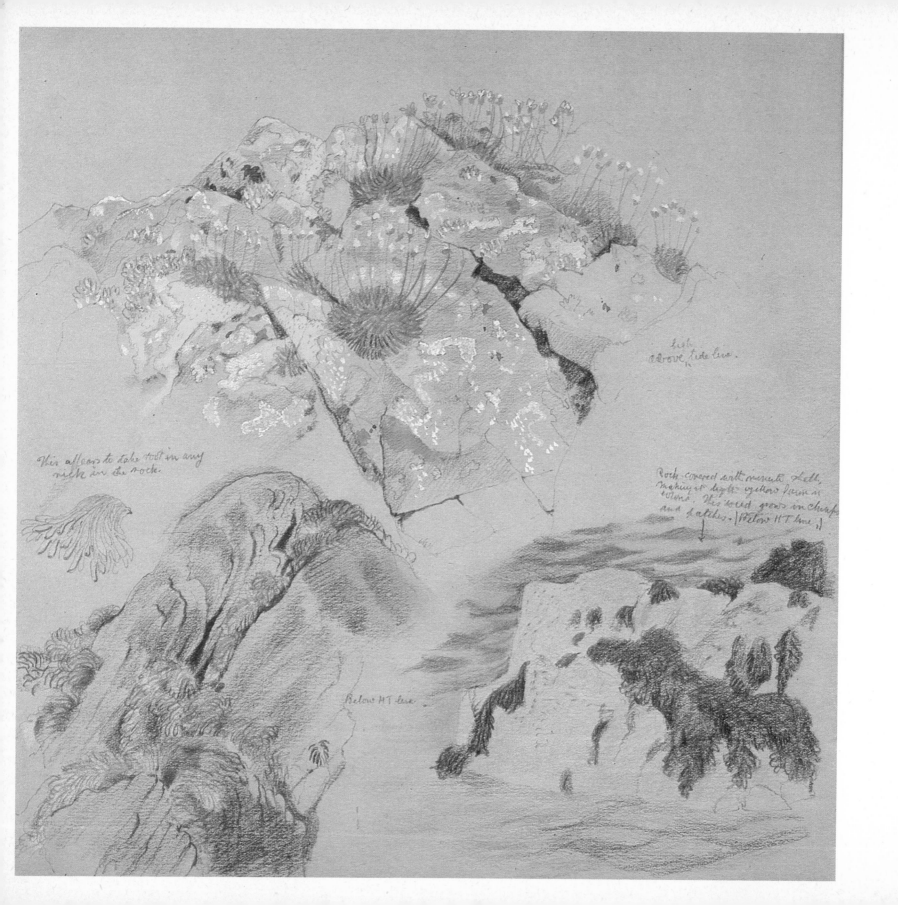

above tide line.

This appears to take root in any
nick in the rock.

Rock covered with minute shells,
making it light yellow from a
colour. This weed grows in clumps
and patches. (Below H.T. line.)

Below H.T. line.

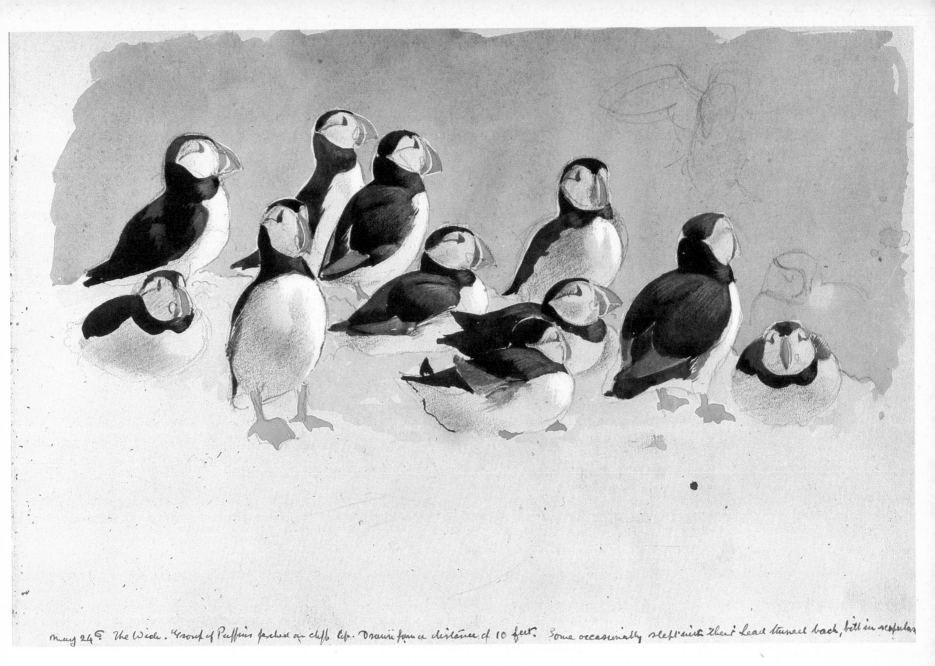

may 24ᵗʰ The Wick. Group of Puffins perched on cliff top. Drawn from a distance of 10 feet. Some occasionally slept with their head turned back, bill in scapulars

102 Three studies of rocks, above and below high tide line, Iona, September 30th 1934.

Tunnicliffe's main note to this drawing in coloured crayon reads:

Rock covered with minute shells, making it light yellow fawn in colour. This weed grows in clumps and patches. (Below high tide line.)

103 Puffin *Fratercula arctica*, The Wick, Skomer Island, May 24th 1949.

Group of Puffins perched on cliff top. Drawn from a distance of 10 feet. Some occasionally slept with their heads turned back, bill in scapulars.

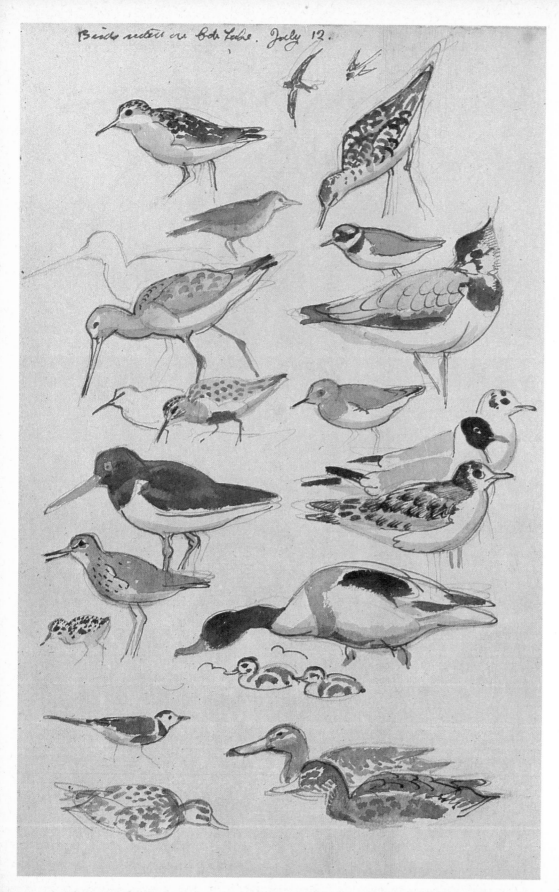

Birds noted on Cob Lake. July 12.

104 Birds noted on Cob Lake, evening, July 12th 1955.

Lake half dried up after a spell of hot weather.

Swifts and Swallows above the lake.

Knot. One only with a pink-russet breast.

Ruff. One, a cripple with left leg joint pointing forward and left foot trailing stiff and useless. Female.

Juvenile Starlings on the mud.

Black T. Godwit. 3 birds. Two grey birds and a smaller russet-breasted one. They have been in the vicinity for some weeks.

At least two Ringed Plover.

A flock of Lapwing, young and old, with a freak bird among them. Where the feathers should have been green only a pale drab to cream colour showed.

A small flock of Dunlin mostly adults with several juveniles.

A family of six Common Sandpipers.

A sprinkling of Oystercatchers which several times indulged in piping parties.

A flock of B. H. Gulls among which were all stages of plumage from full summer to winter with a number of juveniles.

Redshanks—adults, juveniles and a brood of chicks in the sedges.

Shelduck. Two pairs of adults and 42 ducklings which kept on getting mixed up causing much squabbling among the parents.

Several Pied Wags on the mud.

Shovellers, Mallard and Teal, all brown birds with no trace of winter male plumage in any.

105 Curlew *Numenius arquata*, Cefni estuary, Newborough shore, March 17th 1968.

N.W. gale blowing. Two Curlew, one resting on a tump of sedge, the other in the shallows. One noticeably larger than the other, male and female possibly.

Birds noted on Cob Lake, March 17th 1968.

Strong N.W. wind blowing and water very rough.

Teal resting on the bank and under the Cob. They looked like leaden grey stones.

Redshank resting in the shelter of a rush clump. Others were flying about in pairs.

♂ Shelduck walking in the shallows, tail to wind, flank feathers blown forward.

B. H. Gulls rested in a flock on the gravelly spit in what appeared to be shelter.

A solitary Long-tailed duck, diving in the rough water of the lake.

Shelduck seemed to be unaffected by the strong cold wind. They rested, swam and flew aggressively at rival males, and looked fine sculptured shapes. The Long-tailed duck fed in the rougher deeper water with dives which were of long duration.

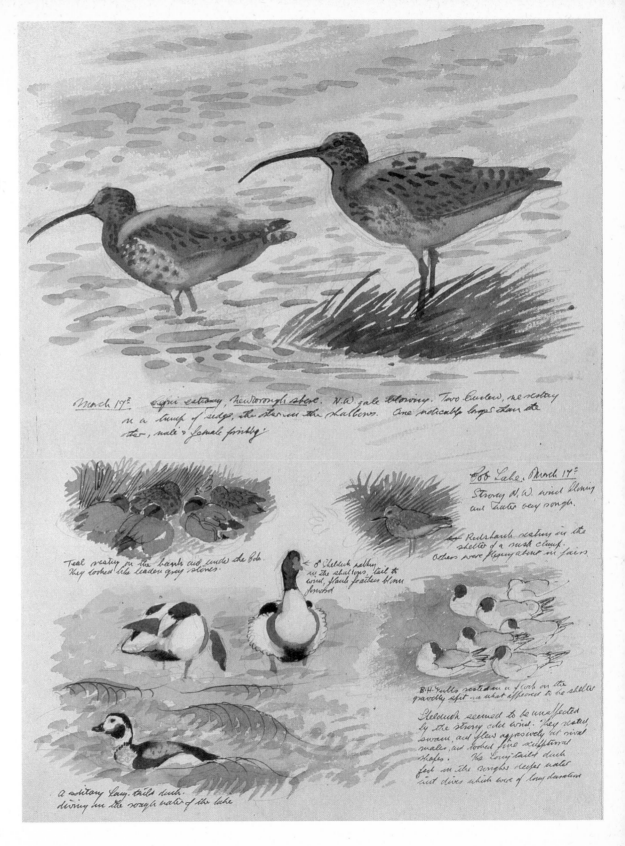

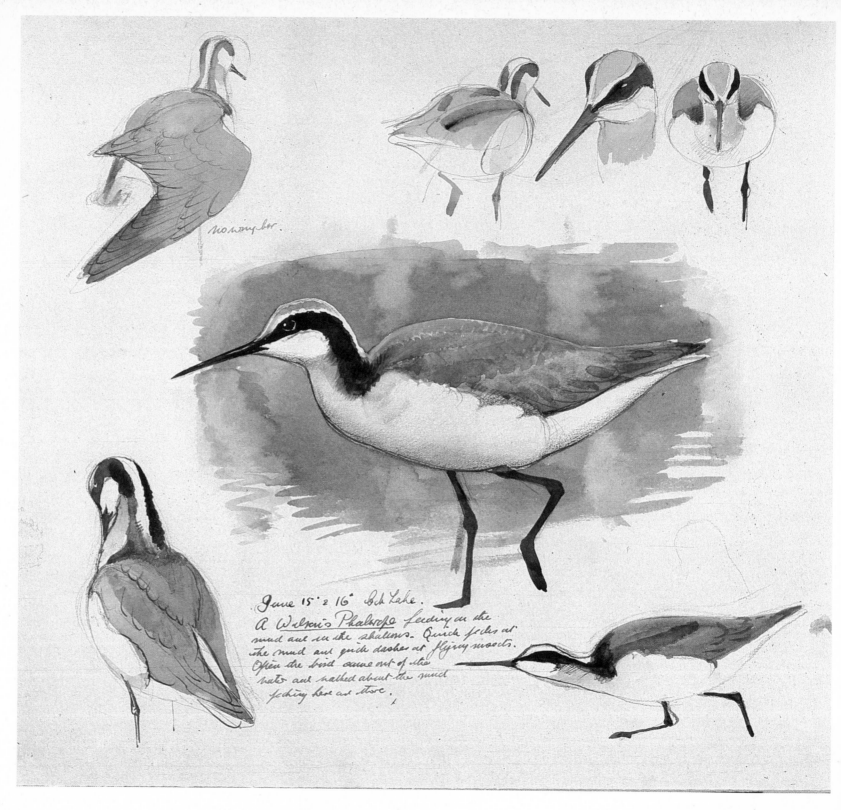

106 and **107** Wilson's Phalarope *Phalaropus tricolor*, Cob Lake, June 15th and 16th 1958.

A Wilson's Phalarope feeding on the mud and in the shallows. Quick pecks at the mud and quick dashes at flying insects. Often the bird came out of the water and walked about the mud pecking here and there.

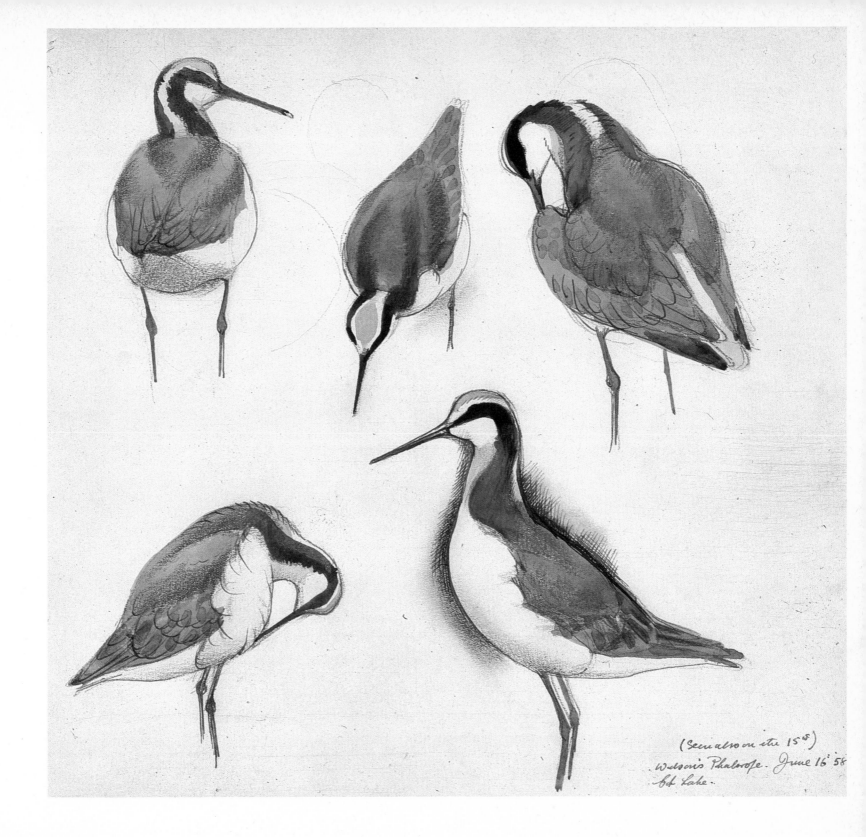

(See also on etc 15ᵗ)

Wilson's Phalarope. June 16 58

At Lake.

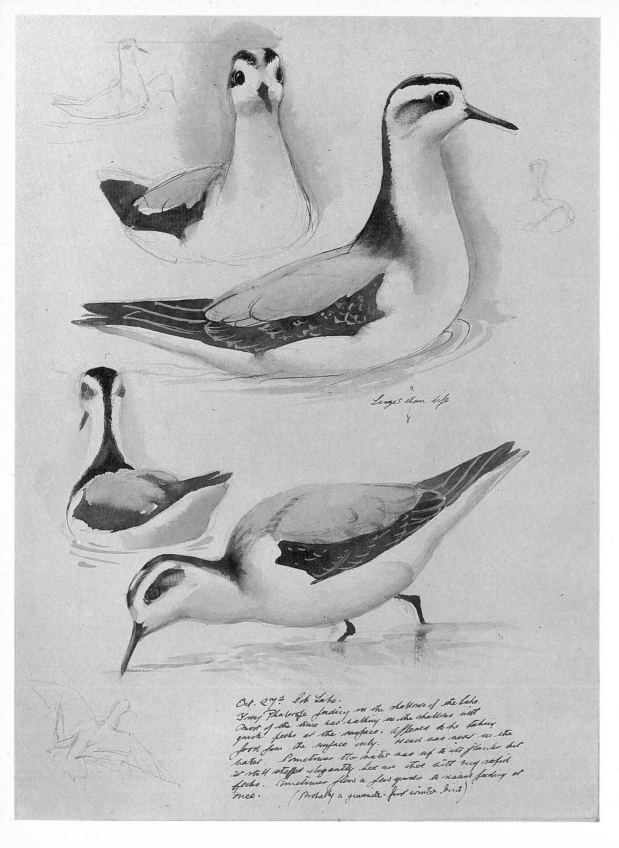

Larger than life

Oct. 27th Cob Lake.
Grey Phalarope feeding in the shallows of the Lake.
Most of the time was walking in the shallows with
quick pecks at the surface. Appeared to be taking
food from the surface only. Head was never in the
water. Sometimes the water was up to its flanks but
it still stepped elegantly here and there with very rapid
pecks. Sometimes flew a few yards to resume feeding at
once. (Probably a juvenile—first winter bird)

108 Grey Phalarope *Phalaropus fulicarius*, Cob Lake, October 27th 1969.

Grey Phalarope feeding in the shallows of the lake. Most of the time was walking in the shallows with quick pecks at the surface. Appeared to be taking food from the surface only. Head was never in the water. Sometimes the water was up to its flanks but it still stepped elegantly here and there with very rapid pecks. Sometimes flew a few yards to resume feeding at once. (Probably a juvenile—first winter bird.)

109 Little Gull *Larus minutus*, Cob Lake, April 20th 1970.

3 Little Gulls sheltering in the lee of the Cob. They had been feeding on Cob Lake. Strong wind blowing and even under the Cob the gulls were buffeted. Tails were carried level with the flights and could scarcely be seen.

N.B. Variation in the amount of dark colour on the head. In this windy weather they were inclined to stand with their heads low, and with tail and wing-tips high.

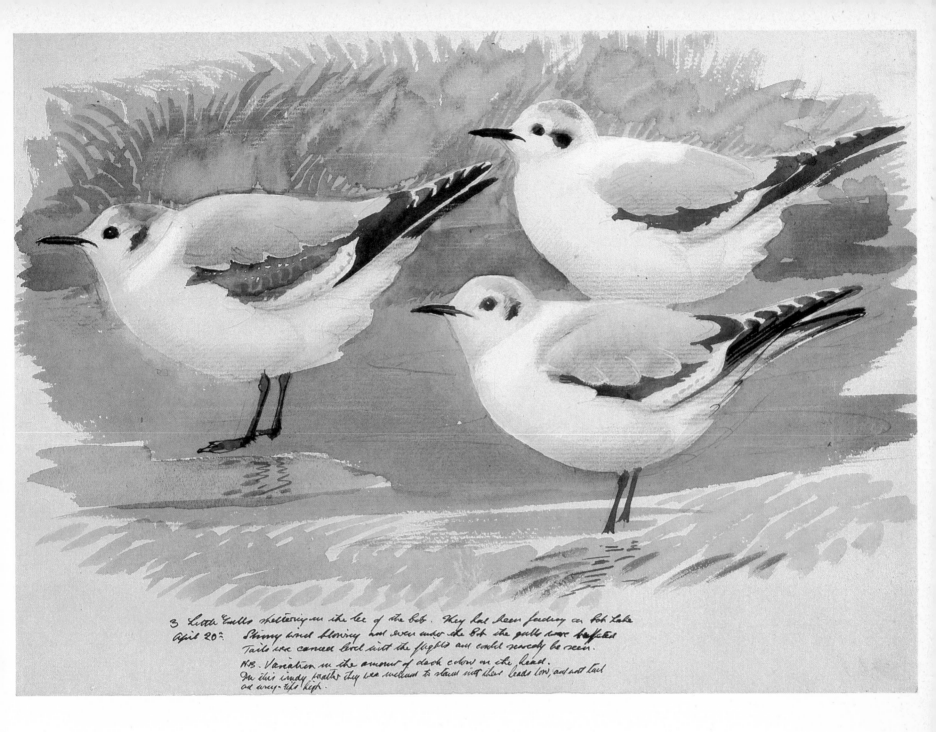

3 Little Gulls sheltering in the lee of the bob. They had been feeding on Pot Lake
April 20th. Stormy wind blowing and even under the Pot the gulls were buffeted
Tails were carried level with the flights and could scarcely be seen.
N.B. Variation in the amount of dark colour on the head.
In this windy weather they were inclined to stand with their heads low, and not tail
or wing-tips high.

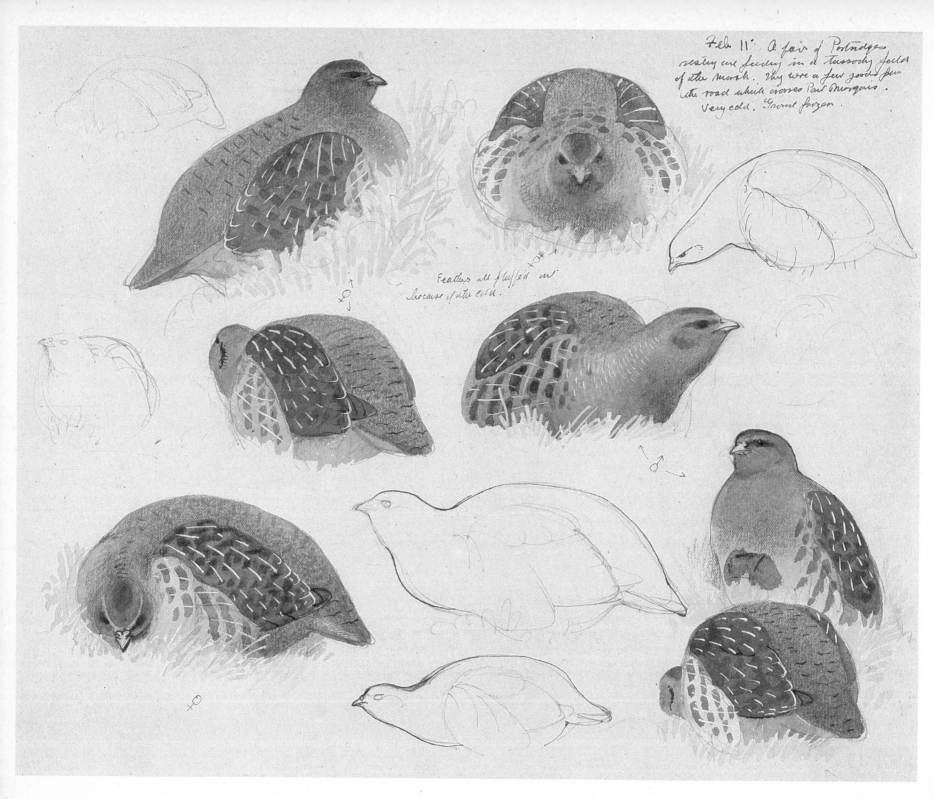

Feb 11th. A pair of Partridges
resting and feeding in a tussocky field
of the marsh. They were a few yards from
the road which crosses Pont Marquis.
Very cold. Ground frozen.

Feathers all fluffed out
because of the cold.

110 Partridge *Perdix perdix*, Pont Marquis,
February 11th 1956.

*A pair of Partridges resting and feeding in a tussocky
field of the marsh. They were a few yards from the road
which crosses Pont Marquis. Very cold. Ground frozen.
Feathers all fluffed out because of the cold.*

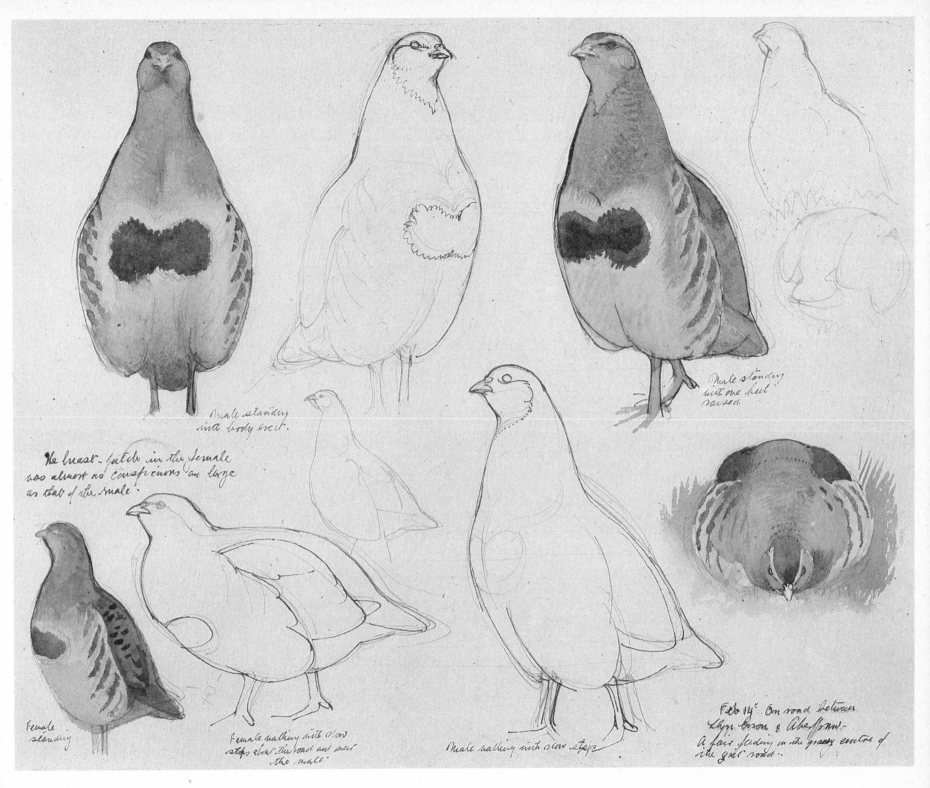

Male standing with body erect.

Male standing with one heel raised.

The breast-patch in the female was almost as conspicuous an large as that of the male.

Female standing

Female walking with slow steps about the road and near the male.

Male walking with slow steps

Feb 14 On road between Llyn Coron & Aberffraw. A pair feeding on the grassy centre of the grit road.

111 Partridge *Perdix perdix*, on road between Llyn Coron and Aberffraw, February 14th 1956.

A pair feeding on the grassy centre of the grit road. The breast patch in the female was almost as conspicuous and large as that of the male.

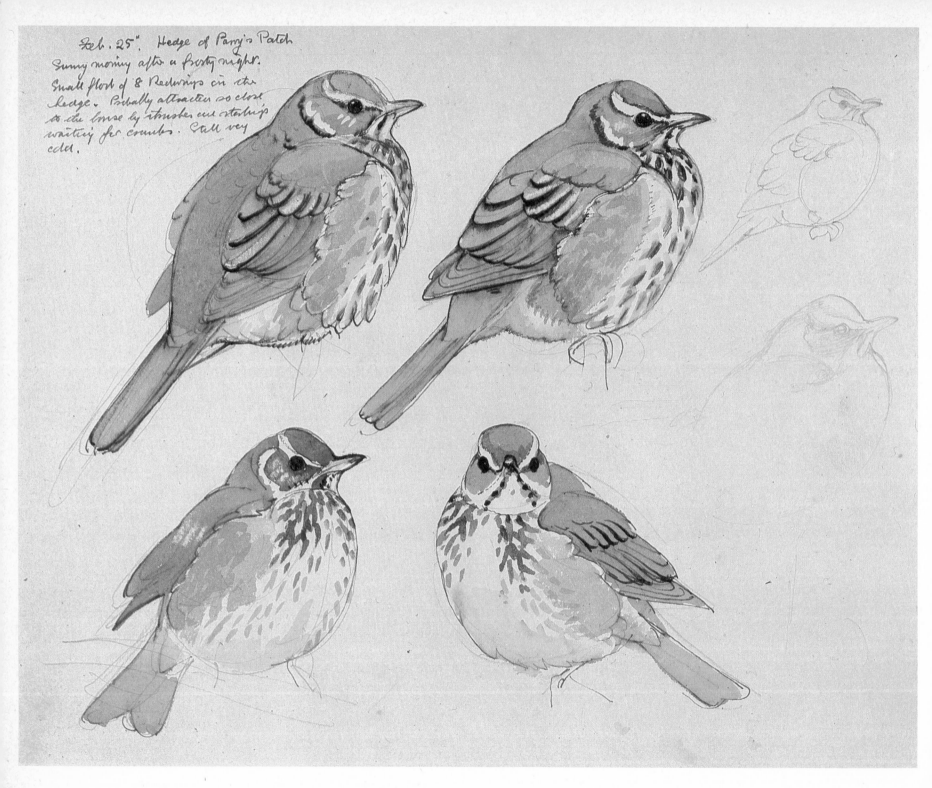

Feb. 25th. Hedge of Parry's Patch
Sunny morning after a frosty night.
Small flock of 8 Redwings in the
hedge. Probably attracted so close
to the house by thrushes and starlings
waiting for crumbs. Still very
cold.

112 Redwing *Turdus musicus*, hedge of Parry's Patch, February 25th 1956.

Sunny morning after a frosty night.

Small flock of 8 Redwings in the hedge. Probably attracted so close to the house by thrushes and Starlings waiting for crumbs.

Still very cold.

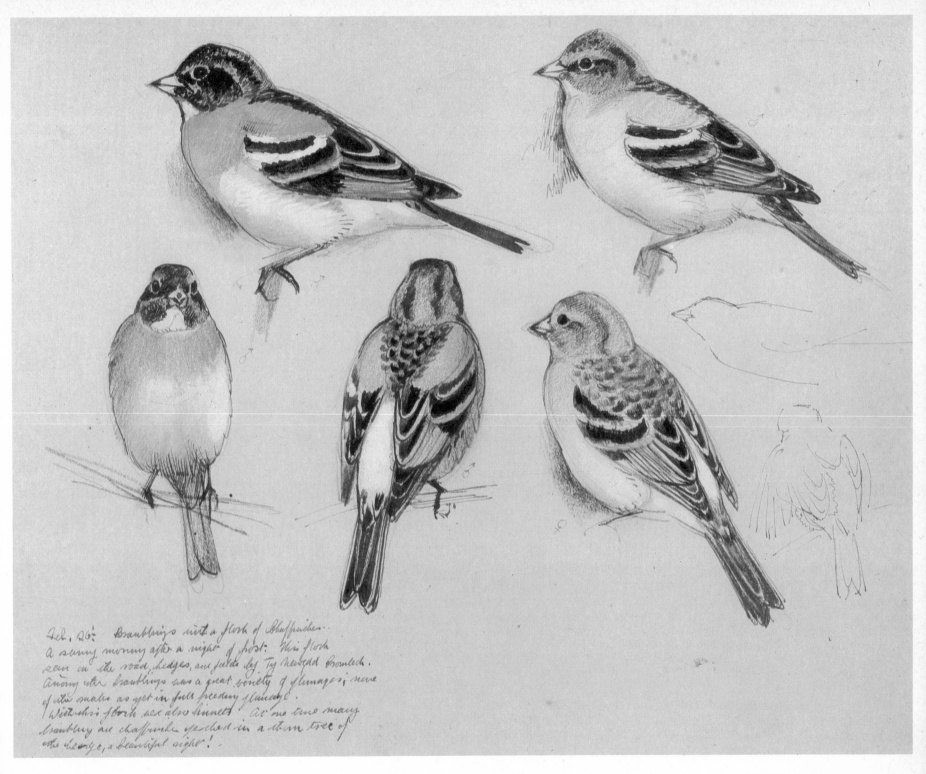

113 Brambling *Fringilla montifringilla*, Ty Newedd Cromlech, February 26th 1956.

Bramblings with a flock of Chaffinches. A sunny morning after a night of frost. This flock seen in the road, hedges and fields by Ty Newedd Cromlech. Among the Bramblings was a great variety of plumages, none of the males as yet in full breeding plumage. With this flock were also Linnets. At one time many Bramblings and Chaffinches perched in a thorn tree of the hedge a beautiful sight!

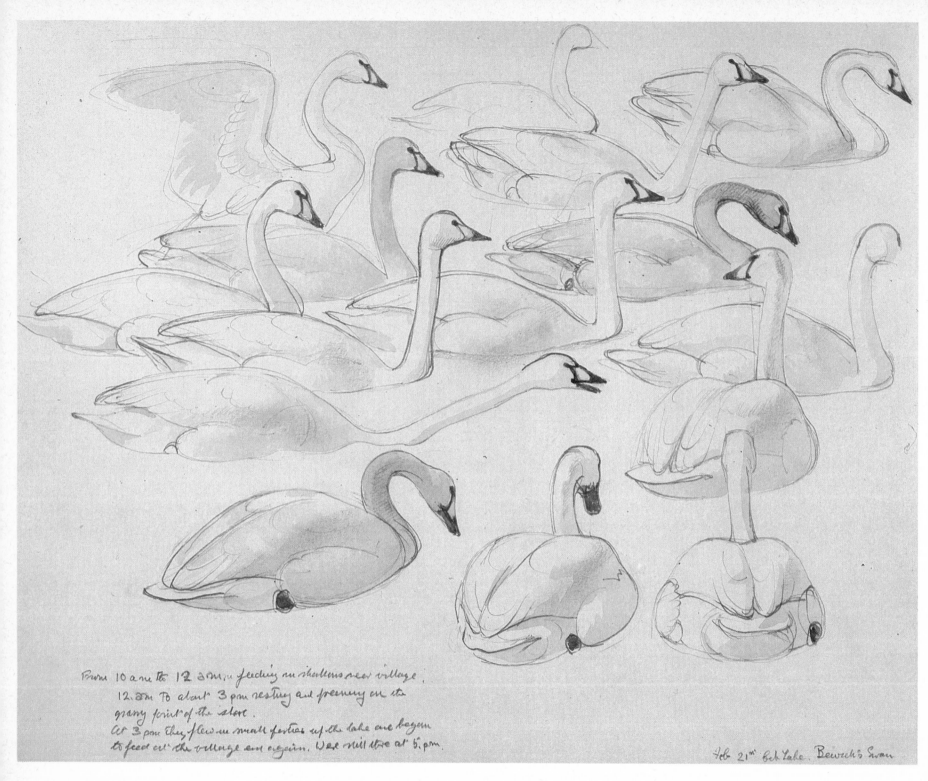

From 10 a.m. to 12 a.m. feeding in shallows near village.
12. a.m. to about 3 pm resting and preening on its
grassy point of the shore.
At 3 pm they flew in small parties up the lake and began
to feed at the village end again. Were still there at 5 pm.

Feb 21st Cob Lake. Bewick's Swan

114 Bewick's Swan *Cygnus bewickii*, Cob Lake,
February 21st 1951.

From 10 am to 12 am feeding in shallows near village.
12 am to about 3 pm resting and preening on the grassy
point of the shore. At 3 pm they flew in small parties up
the lake and began to feed at the village end again. Were
still there at 5 pm.

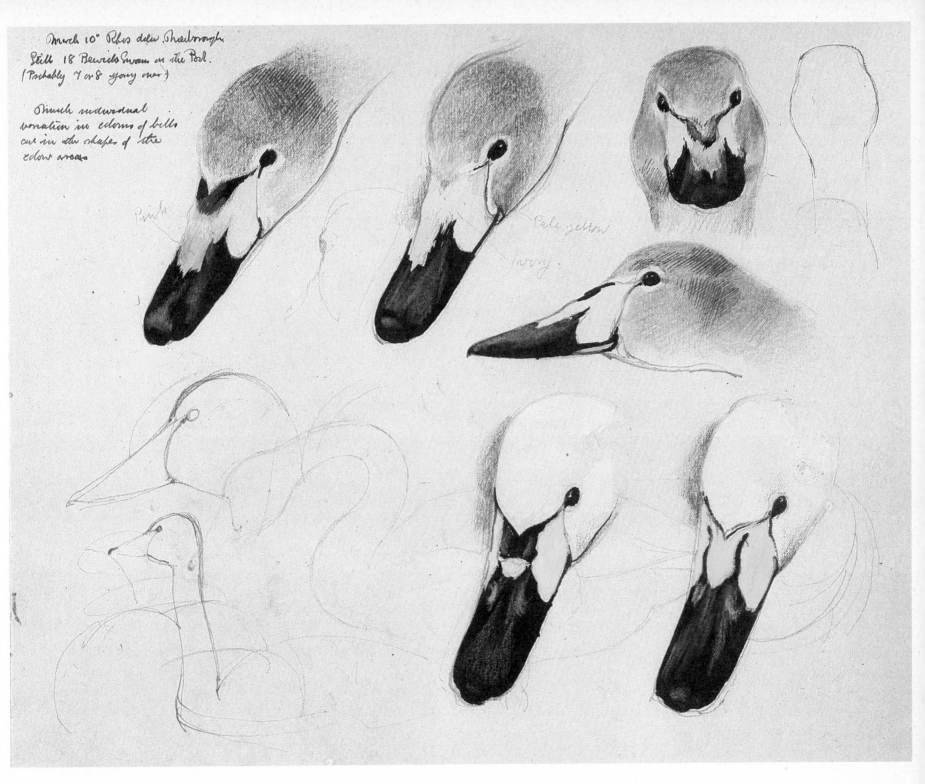

Much 10ᵗʰ Rhos dur Newborough
Still 18 Bewick's Swan on the Pool.
(Probably 7 or 8 young ones.)

Much individual
variation in colours of bills
and in the shapes of the
colour areas.

Pink

Pale yellow
Ivory.

115 Bewick's Swan *Cygnus bewickii*, Rhos, Newborough, March 10th 1956.

Still 18 Bewick's Swans on the Pool. (Probably 7 or 8 young ones.) Much individual variation in colours of bills and in the shapes of the colour areas.

In the early 1960s Bewick's Swans started visiting the Wildfowl Trust at Slimbridge in large numbers and the variation in bill pattern made it possible to identify every bird individually, greatly benefiting the Trust's major continuing study of this species.

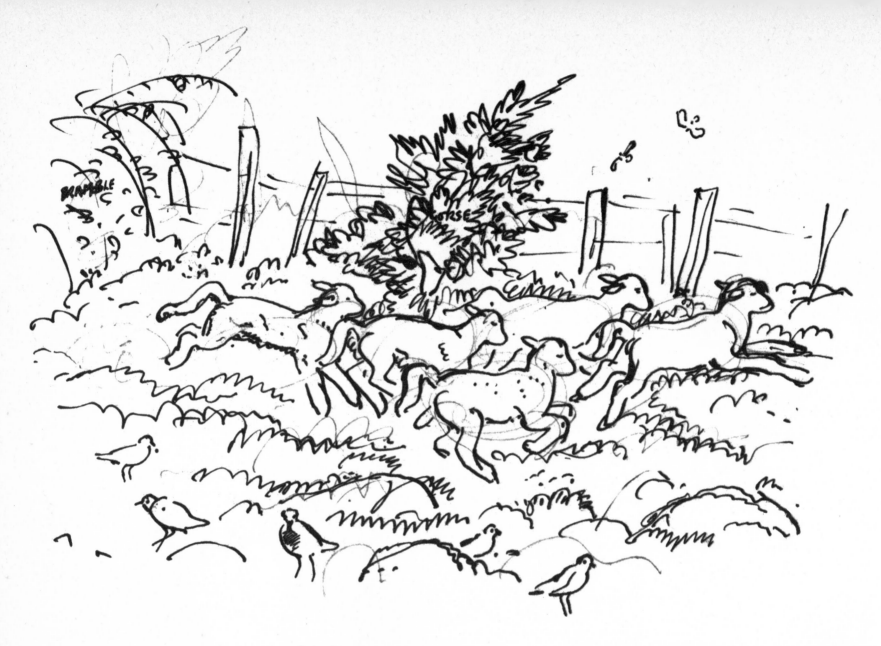

116 Anglesey, evening, March 28th 1956.

Farmyard Field, full of mole-hills. A flock of Golden Plover among the mole-hills and ewes and lambs in the field. Lambs racing along the hedge-bank in galloping groups, first one way, then the other. Sometimes racing among plover causing them to take wing. Lapwings swooping, Redshanks calling and displaying.

This observation probably inspired the memorable watercolour, *Hooligans*, in which three lively lambs are putting up a party of Golden Plovers, exhibited at the Royal Academy in 1975, nearly twenty years later.

117 Garganey *Anas querquedula*, Cob Lake, March 29th 1956.

A few hours after making the previous drawing, Tunnicliffe was at Cob Lake sketching a small party of Garganey, one of the most attractive of the smaller ducks.

Early morning, 5 Garganey feeding with Common Teal. 3 drakes, 2 ducks. Garganey drake noticeably larger than drake Teal.

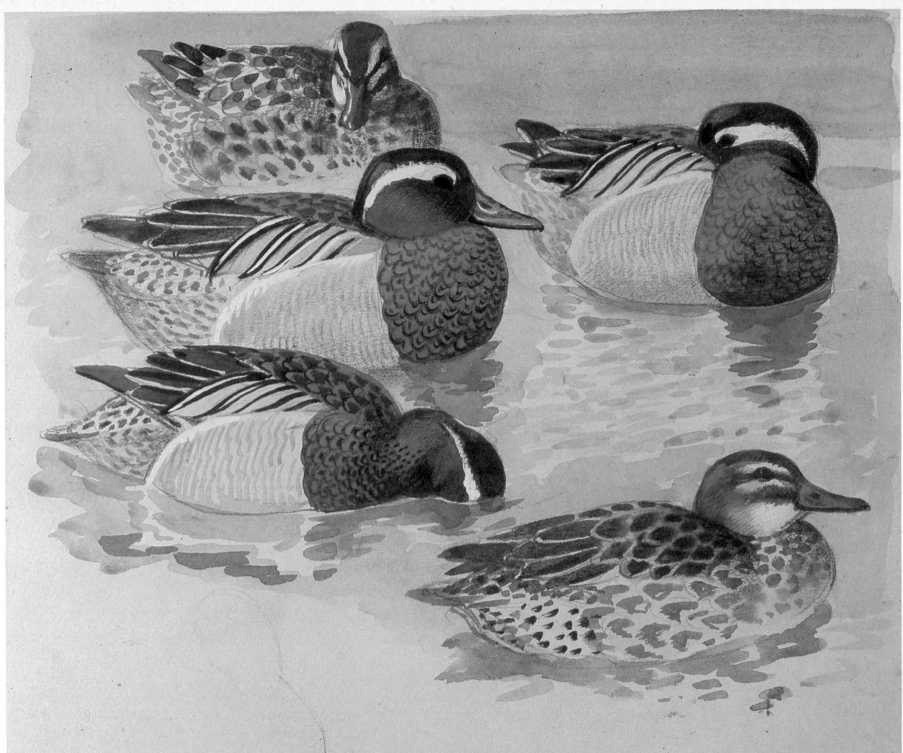

March 29: Ah Labe. Early morning. 5 Garganey feeding with Common Teal
3 drakes. 2 ducks. Garganey drake noticeably larger than drake Teal

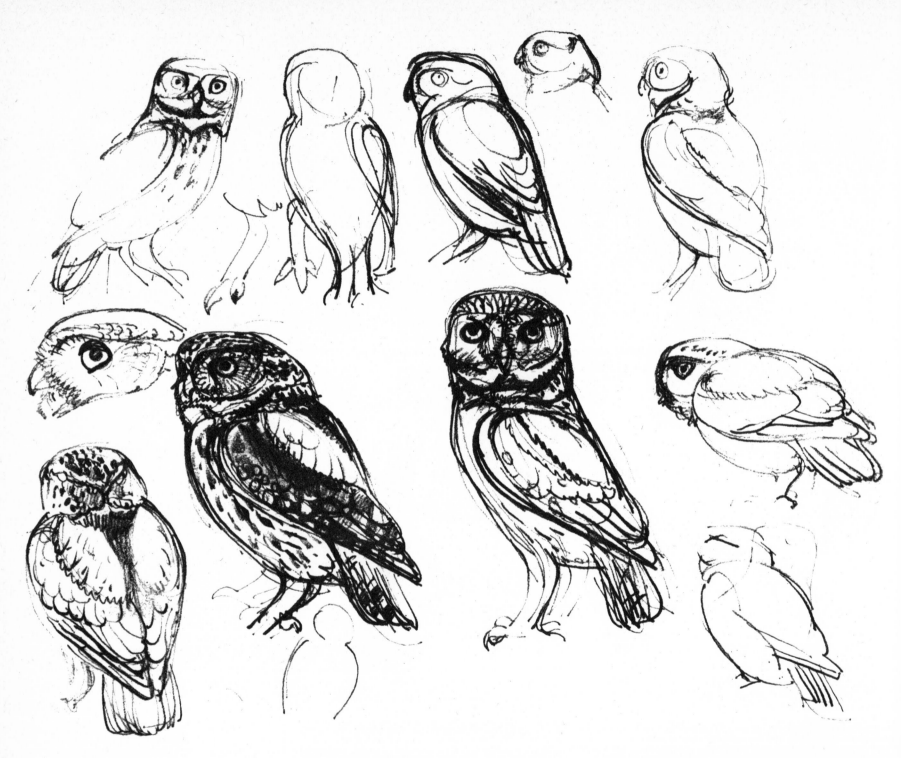

118 Little Owl *Athene noctua*, Shorelands, August 13th 1951.

Tunnicliffe hand-reared this juvenile Little Owl which had been brought to him, too young to fly, in a paper bag by two boys from Capel Manor. It was fed on rabbits and dead birds and by August 15th was strong on the wing and very fit. The main upright pose was adopted when the owl was ready to fly from its perch and often accompanied by a bobbing up and down of head and neck.

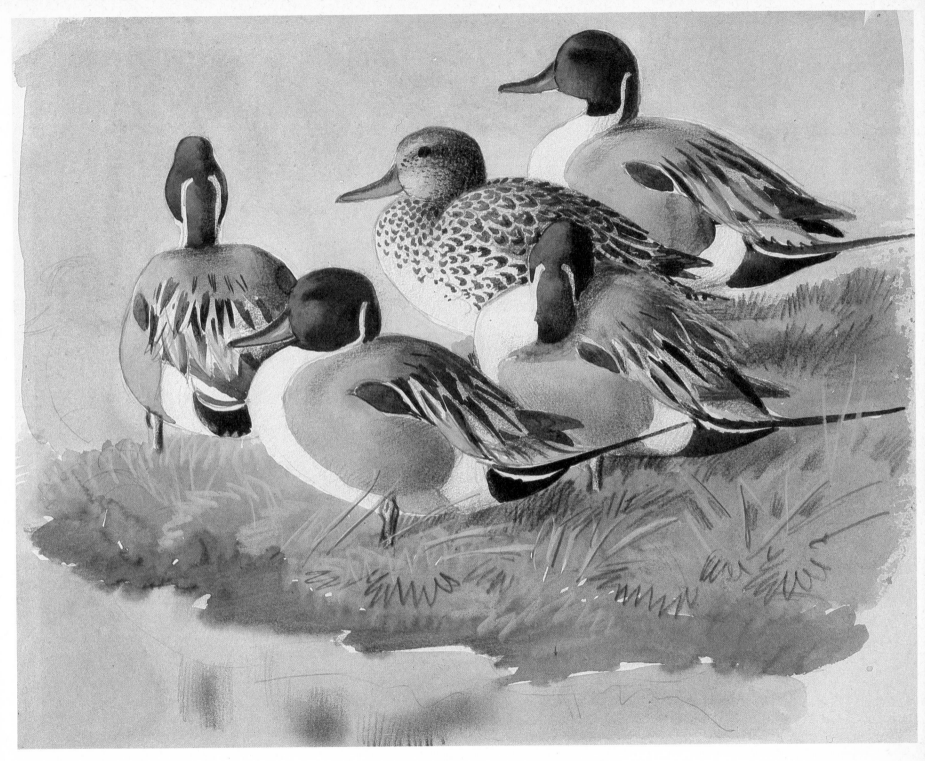

119 Pintail *Anas acuta*, Cob Lake, March 1951.

A party of four drakes and a duck resting on Cob Lake shore in the morning sun. The elegant Pintail is understandably a favourite subject of bird artists and Tunnicliffe was no exception. He made many beautiful compositions of Pintail, inspired by seeing and sketching small groups like this.

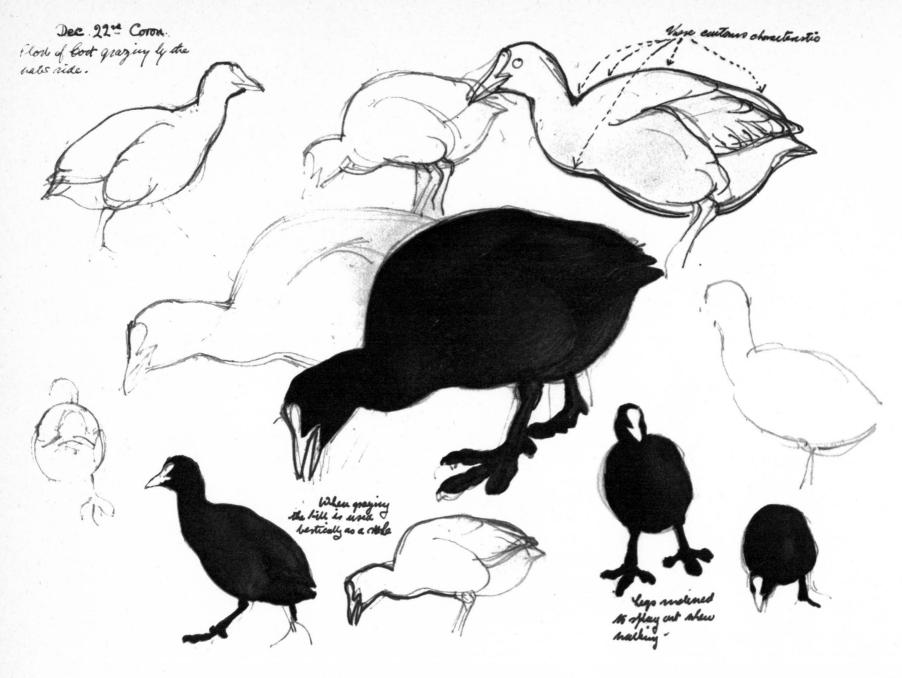

Dec. 22nd Coron.
Flock of Coot grazing by the nabs side.

These contours characteristic

When grazing the bill is used vertically as a rule

Legs inclined to splay out when walking

120 Coot *Fulica atra*, Coron, December 22nd 1947.

A typical page of annotated sketches showing a variety of poses as Coots grazed by the water side. He used his pen to emphasise the pencil drawing (top right), where he refers to the Coot's characteristic contours. He notes that *when grazing the bill is used vertically as a rule*, and that its *legs inclined to splay out when walking.*

121 Wood Sandpiper *Tringa glareola*, Cob Lake,
August 7th 1970.

This fine study of a Wood Sandpiper, feeding in
the sedgy border of Cob Lake, comes from a
sketchbook which Tunnicliffe was using in 1970.
Compare this with the drawing of rocks on Iona
(**102**) done 36 years earlier, in 1934. During this
span his style changed, but there was no
slackening of the acute observation and gifted
draughtsmanship which is a hallmark of his work.

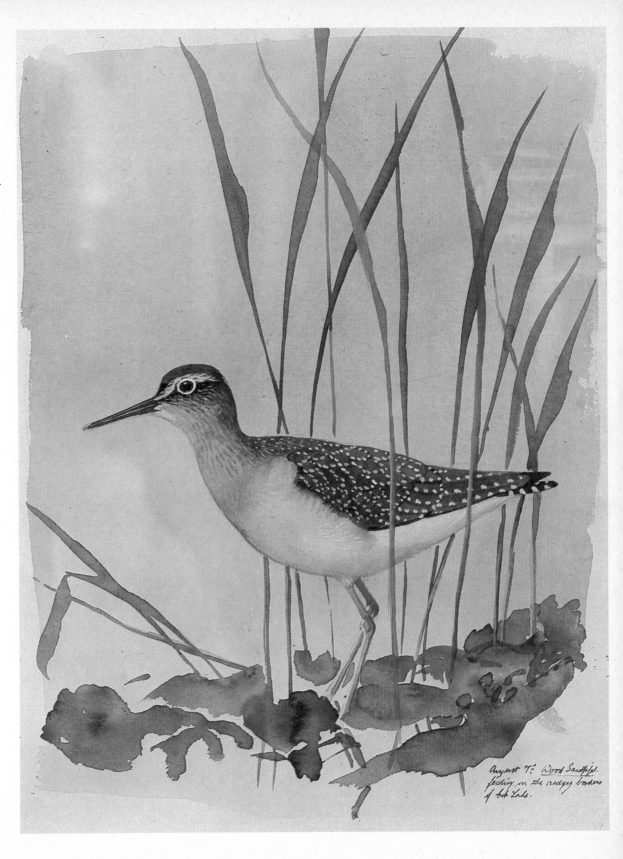

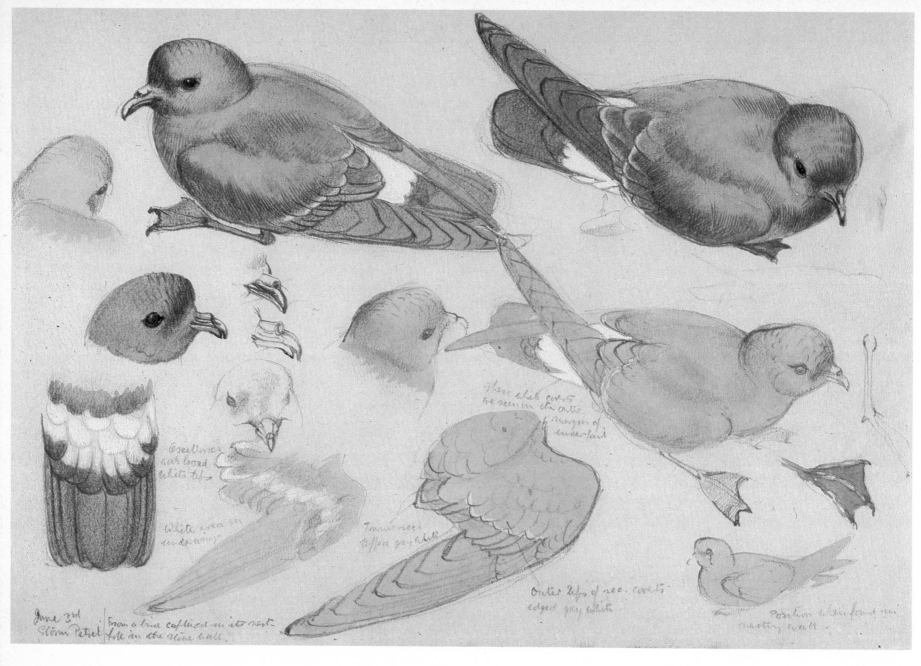

Within the sketch (handwritten annotations):

June 3rd
Storm Petrel

From a bird captured on its nest hole in the stone wall.

Excellence has broad white tips

White area underwing

Tail sees upper grey white

These white coverts be seen on the outer margin of underfail

Outer tips of sec. coverts edged grey white

Position when found in nesting wall

122 Storm Petrel *Hydrobates pelagicus*, Skomer Island, June 3rd 1949.

Tunnicliffe has taken full advantage of a rare opportunity to draw a bird seldom seen at close quarters. Removing a Storm Petrel from its nest-hole in a stone wall, he made careful studies of every part of the bird, knowing from experience just what information he needed for picture making later. If, on returning from the island, he had found the details inadequate, it would have been too late. There could be no going back. Tunnicliffe, as usual, had made his sketches with purpose and to perfection.

Acknowledgements

Quotations from *Shorelands Summer Diary* by C. F. Tunnicliffe are included by permission of Collins; those from *Mereside Chronicle* are included by permission of the Hamlyn Publishing Group Limited. For permission to quote from his autobiography *An Eye for a Bird* published by Hutchinson I am grateful to Eric Hosking O.B.E. Hon F.R.P.S. The BBC and Derek Trimby, producer of *True to Nature*, the TV programme on Tunnicliffe's life, kindly allowed me to quote from transcripts of interviews. Francis Farmar of Christie's helpfully facilitated my study of the sketchbooks while they were in his care. The Medici Society kindly provided material for the painting "Whooper Bathing", reproduced here with their permission. Winwood Reade made many invaluable suggestions for the improvement of my text. I am deeply grateful to David Burnett of Gollancz for letting me make the book as I wanted and for much help and even more patience. My wife Sue gave great support and encouragement while I adopted the unaccustomed role of author.

R. G.

Index